D1444822

In this moving and beautifully written memoir, Christy Cabe shows readers how to find hope and contentment amidst the day-to-day realities of life. She reminds us that joy is not contingent on our circumstances – it is available through Christ in even the deepest and darkest valleys. Your faith will be refreshed as you savor every "morsel" of Christy's inspiring story.

—Jim Daly, President – Focus on the Family

It's people like Christy Cabe who allow us to experience life more deeply through sharing their own experiences. *Brownie Crumbs* opens our hearts and our minds to live and remember. You'll laugh, you'll cry, you'll smile, and you'll sit in awe as you turn the pages. This book connected to my life journey, both on and off the court, and aligns with my desire to search for the good in every situation, and ultimately, to IMPACT the lives of those around me. Thank you, Christy, for such an amazing read!

—Tamika Catchings, former WNBA All-Star and Olympian and author of *Catch A Star*

Brownie Crumbs is a must read memoir. From laugh-out-loud childhood tales to touching stories about loss and leukemia, Christy shows us how our life morsels sustain us through laughter and tears. Through her personal journey, you will learn to savor life—every bite is better than the last!

—Sara Ward, freelance writer and blogger at *PoetsAndSaints.com*

Christy takes you into the heart of loss, leukemia, mold, miscarriage -- and yet what you're left with is a life-affirming sense of God's faithfulness. This book is a sweet reminder to cherish every season of life, even those that aren't ideal, as well as a lesson that earthly life itself is just one season in the larger scheme of things. I enjoyed every morsel of *Brownie Crumbs*!

—Susan Braun, blogger at *Girls In White Dresses*

Christy takes us along on her journey, sharing her most vulnerable life stories. Walk with her as she faces her deepest fears and embraces the heartbreak that leads her to a deeper faith in God. Her humor shines through with a joyful message that reminds us that even in the darkest moments, Jesus offers hope. Christy inspires us all to seize life, the best and worst equally, knowing that as we do, God will sustain us in both.

—Lori Clounie, blogger at *Only God, loriclounie.com*

Christy Cabe is a life-long writer, from her pre-teen journal after early loss to blog updates on her son's cancer journey. In *Brownie Crumbs*, her spiritual memoir, she has mined her story for the lessons learned along the way. Christy doesn't flinch from the truth of the moment, and writes with clarity, humor, and wisdom about the bitter and the sweet.

—Michelle Shappell Harris, MFA

brownie crumbs

and other life morsels

Christy Cabe

Cover Design: Susan Rekeweg

Author Photo: Kraig Cabe

Interior layout and design: Christy Cabe and Susan Rekeweg

Interior photos were provided by Christy Cabe and family

Scripture quotations (unless noted) are taken from the Holy Bible, New International Version®, NIV®. Copyright © 1973, 1978, 1984, 2011 by Biblica, Inc.™ Used by permission. All rights reserved worldwide.

Scripture quotations marked KJV are from the Holy Bible, King James Version.

Printed by CreateSpace, An Amazon.com Company

To Dad and Mom, Dennis and Karin Miller – without your influence and presence in my life, the impact of this story would be greatly diminished. I'm forever grateful.

Kraig – without your support, I probably would have never told this story. Thanks for believing in me, loving me, sharpening me, and for always knowing how to make me laugh. You are the love of my life!

Kids – I wrote this book for you three most of all. I hope you read it some day and realize how much your dad and I love you, and even more, how much God loves you!

And in loving memory of the wonderful woman who gave birth to me and helped to lay the foundation of my life for almost eleven years.
My mom, Mary Sue Miller, 1954-1989

on the menu

foreword

It's rare to find such an honest and beautiful book as the one in your hands right now. Life often hands us lemons and other sour things to digest. How we deal with those times can develop character if we choose wisely. Christy Cabe learned early that choosing to embrace whatever comes our way leads to a life of growth and joy.

I first became acquainted with Christy when she sent me a Facebook message asking if we could talk about the publishing world. I'm always happy to talk about the industry and agreed to meet with her. As soon as I read her proposal, I knew it had great potential to reach hearts and encourage others facing fiery trials. This is a book that needs to be read widely and talked about at great length.

I hope you will read *Brownie Crumbs and Other Life Morsels* with an open heart, ready to learn the secret of a full and joyous life.

This book can change your life if you let it!

Colleen Coble, *USA Today* bestselling author

prologue

brownie crumbs

why they remind me to savor life

It was the last brownie in the pan. Its crumbly consistency, easily falling apart when handled, seemed devastatingly appropriate.

This brownie was the last my mom would make. Once I ate it, it would be gone forever.

Just as she was.

In the days following my mother's sudden and shocking death, I went through many robotic motions.

I made myself climb out of bed. I made myself pull shirts over my swirling head and down over my broken heart. I ate food I couldn't taste, brought by the masses, who were simply desperate to help my dad, brother, and me. Our counter and kitchen table overflowed with casseroles. And with gifts.

It was Easter weekend, when hidden eggs and chocolate bunnies celebrated new life. It was also the week of my eleventh birthday, another apparent reason for celebration and gift giving.

I performed the motions of accepting these celebrations dictated by the calendar. I made myself smile and express my gratitude to the givers.

The gifts were fine. A china doll in a blue satin dress stood stiff and stoic in her white wire stand. A teddy bear with fake flowers around its neck and rough fur that scratched my face. Barbies. Candy. Easter goodies.

I forced myself to accept these things, to eat the treats, but my efforts to appreciate them were only for the sake of others. I was trying to prove that I was "okay," and that I was able to feel some comfort and happiness in these tokens of support.

But as I sat alone on the couch in our family room one afternoon, I *wanted* to eat that last brownie more than anything. Because it was now or never. And I certainly wasn't doing it for anyone else. I was doing it for me.

I sat in the quiet room in blessed solitude with my legs folded beneath me on the couch. I held the brownie on a napkin as if it were made of glass and could shatter with the slightest motion.

And I took a bite.

I slowly chewed that bite, and then the next, and the next. I swallowed the final morsel. I had savored every bit, and when a tiny crumb had fallen onto my white napkin, I had pinched it between my finger and thumb and brought it to my lips.

I would not allow even the tiniest crumb to be forgotten.

This explains a lot.

As I reflect on the eating of that sacred brownie, I realize that moment represents the way I live.

In the thousands of days since the brownie, I've encountered countless reasons to celebrate and a few reasons to mourn.

I've tasted sweet moments and winced at bitter ones. Some days were downright bland.

But I've tried to savor most.

If a moment is in danger of being lost to apathy, distraction, or ingratitude, I pry and pinch until I grasp it again. I find value in even the tiniest of crumbs.

With eyes wide open and taste buds watering, I live ready to savor the days, the hours, the moments. I strive to remember the morsels of the life I've been served.

And it brings me pleasure to share these memories with you. In doing so, I pray these morsels will whet your appetite and challenge and encourage you to savor your own. May you find joy in both the scrumptious and the bitter. May you find peace in the bland. And most of all, may you see hope in the crumbs.

Bon appétit.

one

animal crackers

why they are not the only delicious memory from my childhood

My feet bounced in front of me as I kicked my legs while riding in the backseat. The little red Mary Jane shoes I had so desperately wanted, and had used my own money to purchase, were accompanied by a pair of folded-over, lace-edged socks. From my seat, I could see the dashboard, along with the backs of Mom's and Dad's heads, as we drove along the country road with my aunt and uncle, who were sitting on each side of me.

It is one of those memories that has crossed the fuzzy boundary between something I actually remember and a story I've heard so many times.

I do remember my Sunday school teacher's words from just a few days earlier. I'd taken them to heart. In fact, I wasn't sure she should have told us kids all of the details she did, but even though I was the pastor's kid, I really didn't feel I had any power to stop her. Now the images stuck in my head.

She had told us about Hell.

Wide-eyed, I sat on the little metal folding chair in the basement of the church and listened in horror as she described a place that was hot and dark and yucky. I decided it sounded horrible in Hell, and kind of sad, too.

I kept my thoughts to myself for a few days. With all the other things I had to think about, such as Holly Hobbie and the Care Bears, I tried not to let it bother me. At least I knew what Hell was like now, in case there was ever a quiz.

As the car bumped down the road, I watched the scenery outside the window. I liked the cows and the barns and the big stone farmhouses we passed on the mountain roads of Pennsylvania.

We drove into the town of Carlisle, where my aunt and uncle were living. I loved spending time with them and was happy they lived just about forty minutes from our home in Chambersburg. As we entered the small town I continued my study of all that passed by my window.

The grown-ups were talking about whatever it is that grown-ups talk about. Boring.

And then I saw it.

A building that made my mouth drop open in disbelief. It was old and falling down in weird angles instead of making a good rectangle shape as it should. What remained of the walls was blackened and burned in places. It was dark and yucky and it looked horrible and kind of sad.

Just like...

"Hey, look!" I said to my grown-ups. "That place looks like Hell!"

Sometimes grown-ups silently look around really slowly at each other as if they hear something kids can't. My parents and my aunt and uncle did. They all looked as though they didn't feel well. Were they carsick?

Then they stared at me.

I could tell from their squished-up faces and open mouths that they didn't approve of what I'd just said.

Huh? I was just pointing out an obvious observation. That building looked just like the Hell my Sunday school teacher had described. Weren't they glad I had changed the conversation to a church topic?

"What do you mean, Honey?" my mom sweetly asked from her spot in the passenger seat.

Geesh, I thought. *Now I have to explain this to four grown-ups who should be smarter than this! My daddy and my uncle are even preachers, for goodness' sake!*

So I explained what my Sunday school teacher had told me about Hell, and wasn't it obvious that the old, broken building looked just like that horrible place?

The grown-ups all breathed out a lot of air and then smiled. They once again looked at each other as if they were talking without words.

I was just a kid bouncing her Mary Janes in the backseat of a car. I was no smarty-pants, but at least that day on the road I was able to teach my grown-ups something I thought they should have already known.

It's a good thing I paid attention in Sunday school.

*   *   *

Our split-level brick house, with big white pillars on both sides of the front porch, sat directly across Black Gap Road from Mt. Pleasant Church. The church was also built of red brick and sported similar white pillars that stood like proud watchmen beside the large wooden front doors. From my front yard, I could look across the street at the church's beautiful entrance, the Pennsylvania mountains painting a majestic backdrop. I lived in this beautiful setting for seven years, from the age of two until a few months after my ninth birthday.

My dad's work commute rarely required a car, as he'd cross the busy street to his office and walk home again for lunch. I loved being allowed to go to the church with him and explore the empty classrooms, to run freely in the echoing gymnasium. But I could never cross the street on my own. This was made very clear.

My dad had used blue spray paint to mark a line on our driveway, which I was never to cross without an adult. I would ride my bike in circles, but would not dare approach the blue line lest I break the rule and ensure punishment. Even more than the punishment, I dreaded disappointing my parents, or anyone else for that matter.

Our home sat in front of a sprawling back yard bordered by a chain link fence. A safe haven for playing on the swing set, chasing the dogs, or setting up house with imaginary friends.

The name Mt. Pleasant suited the place. Life was pleasant there.

Having been born in Huntington, Indiana, when my dad was finishing his masters in ministry at Huntington College, I was technically a "Hoosier," but Pennsylvania life was all I knew. I had moved to Chambersburg at just four months old when my dad began serving as the associate pastor at a large church in town. The three of us lived in an apartment over the church offices. I said my first word, "birdie," after watching the birds outside our second story window. After a couple of years, Dad received an offer to pastor a church of his own, Mt. Pleasant. A short time later, when I was four, my brother, Nathan, came along.

Our little family of four lived in the Mt. Pleasant parsonage and enjoyed a good life in the Quaker State. My dad and my uncle would hunt. My mom canned the vegetables my Dad grew in his large garden. Nate and I played for hours in the basement.

My Sunday school teachers were also my friends with whom I would play Rummikub at summer family camp at Rhodes Grove Campground. I sang a duet with my mom at Christmastime called "The Gift Goes On," and our voices filled the beautiful sanctuary with the overlooking balcony.

My friend, Danae, and I would explore her family farm and swim in her grandma's pool where she attempted to teach me how to dive. Another girlfriend, Jamie, and I enjoyed slumber parties and playing at each other's houses. Her mom was an artist and allowed us to paint white porcelain figurines in her basement, an activity that quickly became one of my favorite pastimes.

My school days at Scotland Elementary were filled with the smell of Elmer's glue and cafeteria food. My mom brought my little brother in to my kindergarten class for show-and-tell.

My childhood was charmed.

And even the moments that brought pain didn't dampen my pleasant life.

*   *   *

My friends and I called it Gremlin Park. That wasn't its real name, but we thought it was appropriate after hearing spooky noises there one evening that reminded us of the creepy little creatures we'd seen in the popular movie.

I was there with my parents and toddler Nate one evening, a fun family outing to the park that ended sooner than planned.

I had walked carefully across a balance beam, a skill I was proud of for being a first grader. Apparently, I had good balance. At least on the beam.

After jumping off the beam, my feet hit the slippery grass, causing me to fall backward. My right arm landed behind me. I tried to break my fall, but broke my arm instead. Both bones in my arm had snapped and my elbow had been displaced. My parents rushed me to the hospital and I underwent surgery to set my bones. Then I lay in a hospital bed with my right arm in a full cast and hanging in traction above my bed.

The worst part wasn't the pain. It wasn't the heavy plaster cast that stretched from my palm to my shoulder. With my arm in traction, my right thumb couldn't reach my mouth.

As a first grader, I still sucked my thumb.

Maybe this would do the trick. My parents had tried the bitter-flavored nail polish. I sucked it right off. They tried promising toys if I quit. My first grade teacher even slapped my hand during reading group time as I sneaked my thumb into my mouth. I was humiliated, but just couldn't give it up. It was my security.

Now I was like an addict trying to quit cold turkey at a rehab center. I couldn't reach my thumb while it hung in traction. And my left hand just didn't taste the same.

I began to learn that being forced to give up something I loved, something that offered comfort and security, hurts. And that I couldn't control everything that happened to me.

What I could control was how I handled being "one-armed" at school. There were some tasks to which I could adapt on my own, and other tasks, like carrying my lunch tray, that required asking a friend for help. I was willing to at least give everything a try with one arm, and I was also willing to admit when it wasn't working and reach out for help.

I also learned how to write quite well with my left hand. It wasn't as pretty as my right-handed penmanship, but it worked. I found that just because something is not ideal doesn't mean it is not okay.

My arm healed well and my cast was removed weeks later. But, I began to file a few lessons in my head. The first of which was to avoid balance beams.

*   *   *

Our neighbors were out of town and had asked our family to feed their dog while they were away. I was very comfortable around dogs because my dad had been breeding Labrador Retrievers for a few years and we almost always had dogs at our house. Being nipped by a sharp-toothed puppy was a common occurrence.

I had walked over to the neighbors' yard with Dad and was planning to help him with the feeding. I waited in the yard as Dad started into the house to grab the dog food. The neighbor dog was big and snarly, and I wanted to keep my distance because I wasn't sure he would be as friendly as our Labradors. I figured I was safe because the dog was on a chain and he was at the end of his reach.

Only, he wasn't.

As my dad walked away, the dog sensed its chance and it lunged at me. Before I knew it, I was lying on my back with the dog's face against my own. The pain above my eye was piercing.

My dad came running and threw the dog off of me. He picked me up and ran home where he and Mom sat me on the bathroom counter and cleaned up the blood. They feared my eye had been damaged severely.

When the blood was cleared away, it became evident that only the skin on my eyelid had been broken. My vision was unaffected, and I didn't even require stiches.

I was fortunate. It could have been much worse.

I have a scar above my left eye to this day, but I do not have a fear of dogs.

When the dog bites, it doesn't have to keep you down for long.

*   *   *

Darkness covered us. Our campout was well underway, and I snuggled in my sleeping bag with heavy eyes. Granted, we'd only gone as far as the backyard, but sleeping in a tent all night was a pretty big deal to a little girl.

I tried to still the thoughts racing in my brain, and I tried to still my wiggles as well. But I just couldn't. Sleep wasn't happening on this hard ground where cold earth crept through my covers and strange, scary noises echoed.

And then suddenly I knew what would help me fall asleep.

I stretched out my little hand.

Beside me lay my father in his sleeping bag. I couldn't see him, but I knew he was there. What I wanted to know was whether or not he was facing me.

Was his face turned toward me?

I reached into the darkness and found his face. I touched his warm nose and forehead and patted his cheeks.

"What are you doing?" his whispered voice cut through the darkness.

"Daddy, I just wanted to make sure your face was looking at me. Now I can go to sleep."

I smiled and slid my arms back into the warmth of my sleeping bag.

I had found my peace.

Maybe that is why today, as a grown woman, I find comfort in the words of the priestly blessing recorded in Numbers 6:24-26: "The Lord bless you and keep you; the Lord make his face shine on you and be gracious to you; the Lord turn his face toward you and give you peace."

My daddy was looking at me in the darkness. Even if I couldn't see him, I knew he was there.

*   *   *

If you asked me as a child what I wanted to be when I grew up, you probably would have gotten a short list in response.

First of all, I wanted to be a wife and a mommy. I already had adopted a Cabbage Patch kid named Carissa Renee, and that was going pretty well. Her beautiful yarn hair and sweet baby powder scent made me swell with motherly pride. I later adopted a son named Irving Michael. He was bald and took a permanent pacifier, and he was a precious addition to my little nest. Motherhood seemed to suit me so far.

I also liked to mother my little brother. And by "mother" I mean boss around. I was building a well-rounded skill set. I was so excited to have a husband and kids someday. I just needed to grow up first.

But I had other jobs that I dreamed of "outside the home." Vocationally, I wanted to be a Sunday school teacher. I had no idea that this didn't actually pay, or that any job paid, for that matter. Who cared about bills? Who knew that it took actual money to keep the lights turned on at home? I thought people pretty much chose to work wherever sounded fun. I liked my Sunday school teachers, had fun there, and thought I could take over the flannel graph for them some day.

I also liked the thought of being a nurse after spending time in the hospital with my broken arm. Helping someone in pain appealed to me. That, and I was really intrigued by the mauve-colored water jug that accompanied my hospital meal tray. When the jug was tipped to pour the water, the little flap over the spout opened. When you sat the jug upright, the lid fell back over the hole. Amazing. I figured if I were a nurse, I'd get one of these for my very own.

Finally, and maybe the career I most often mentioned to my parents, was the desire to work in one of the Pennsylvania Turnpike tunnels. We would take the Turnpike to Indiana to visit my grandparents, or for other travel. I enjoyed the trips, and the accompanying snacks. Red boxes of animal crackers with little string handles and pictures of circus animals on the outside were some of my favorites. I'd rip open the brown bag inside the box that kept the soon-to-be soggy morsels fresh. The aroma of ginger and sugar filled my little nose. I was well-fed and equipped for tunnel travel.

These wondrous tunnels allowed us to drive straight through the mountain instead of over it. Driving through solid rock? It was as if we possessed a superpower. Secondly, the world grew dark, even in the middle of the bright afternoon, when cars entered the tunnel. Signs advised drivers to remove their sunglasses before entering.

The fluorescent lights on the ceiling would cause brief patches of light to flow through the car. I was sure Han Solo experienced this same thing on the Millennium Falcon when he put her in hyper-drive.

But most of all, I loved the tunnels for the service doors buried within the otherwise bare concrete walls. Oh, how I wanted to go through one! What was on the other side? I imagined a beautiful world of offices where lucky people, who were chosen to work in the tunnel, took their lunch breaks and gazed at the mountainous scenery beside their desks. It didn't matter what kind of work those people did in their tunnel offices. Sign me up.

I was pretty happy with my career options.

The future looked as bright as the light at the end of the tunnel.

*   *   *

I walked down the aisle in a long white dress with a satin belt. He walked beside me in his suave grey suit. He was handsome and my long blonde hair cascaded down my back.

When we reached the front of the large sanctuary, we went through the motions everyone had practiced the evening before at the rehearsal.

After the ceremony, I stood with loved ones and sobbed. It had been a beautiful wedding, but I was devastated, nonetheless.

"Christy, what is wrong?" they asked.

Obviously, I was disappointed, but I didn't want them to be as well. I considered keeping the pain to myself. I really just wanted to please everyone and for us all to be happy.

Finally, I worked up the nerve to tell the truth.

"I didn't want to marry that boy!" I sobbed.

They smiled, patting me on the shoulder and enfolding me in warm hugs. Then they told me the truth. I hadn't married him.

I was the flower girl and he was the ring bearer.

*   *   *

Life in Pennsylvania had made for a happy childhood. Mom had been able to stay home full-time with Nate and me while Dad pastored. Although our house was decorated simply, it welcomed and comforted us. Homemade birthday meals, themed birthday cakes, and family gathered around the table built memories as sweet as my tunnel-traveling animal crackers.

Mom was always very loving and well respected at the church. She taught women's Bible classes and was an excellent teacher. Gentle, sweet, and godly are words that describe her well.

Dad was also teaching Bible classes at the church with a curriculum he had written to teach a survey of Scripture. His material caught on well.

So well, it brought about a shift in our family life.

The headquarters of our denomination were located in Huntington, Indiana. Their Director of Church Services contacted Dad and proposed a job involving traveling to churches and training their pastors in his curriculum, called *Grow in His Word*, so that each church could in turn teach their own people.

The job was enticing, and Dad accepted.

I completed the third grade, and that following summer, we loaded the moving truck and headed back to Huntington, Indiana, the city where I was born.

Back home again in Indiana, we settled in a small house in a neighborhood called Zahm Lake. My new bedroom was pink and grey with wallpaper on only one wall, a feature I thought to be quite modern and amazing in design.

I started fourth grade at my new elementary school and my brother started kindergarten that year. I liked my new school, and thrived there both academically and socially.

More changes came our way with Dad's new travel schedule. He visited many different churches and cities throughout each month, teaching and training church leaders about discipleship.

Mom and Nate and I often attended church alone, both on Sunday mornings and Wednesday evenings. College Park United Brethren Church was only ten minutes from our house and held special memories for my parents as it is where they were married after their sophomore years at Huntington College. The campus sits a block from the church.

College Park Church had a front entrance complete with large white pillars, much like those that stood at the entrance of Mt. Pleasant. It seemed to me that all churches of any significance must have pillars.

Mom took a part-time job at Huntington College, working as an administrative assistant in the Graduate School of Christian Ministries. So, she was mostly gone while Nate and I were at school. One day I stayed home sick from school, and Mom had to go to work. I was left alone for a few hours and was totally fine with that until two strangers rang my doorbell. I peeked through the front window and, not recognizing either man, decided not to answer the door. Then, in a move that both surprised and terrified me, the men walked around the outside of our house and onto our newly constructed three-seasons room where they sat around our patio table and held a conversation. I slithered on my stomach through the kitchen and into the family room where I was able to see what these strangers were doing without being seen myself. I quietly grabbed the phone and called my Mom at work, but no one answered. I found out later most of the staff were attending a chapel on campus.

I had an idea. Pastor Kent Maxwell lived in my neighborhood. I didn't know him well, but I figured a pastor would help. I called and he came quickly to my rescue. After confronting the men, it turns out that they were from the company that had recently built our room addition and they were coming to inspect it and see how the project turned out. When they thought no one was home, they had let themselves onto the porch and sat for a moment to talk. Our embarrassment was mutual.

I was relieved. But mostly, I was thankful that our new friends and neighbors would be there to help when we called.

life morsel: Just because something is not ideal doesn't mean it is not okay.

My mother, Mary, holding
me as a toddler

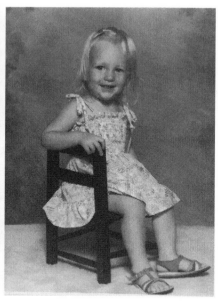

Me, about one year old

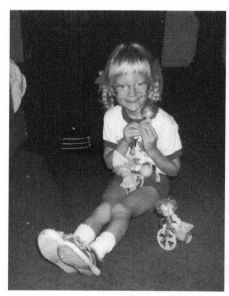

A happy kid!

Listening intently to my Sunday
school teacher as a young girl

Walking down the aisle

With my little brother

Getting a new bike! I was careful
not to ride it past the spray-painted
line on the driveway

Our family. If you look
closely, you can see my right
arm is in a cast

two

deli ham

why I don't care to eat it anymore

I panicked. I should have known what to do, but instead I froze in fear. My dad was shouting at me to call 911 and even though I was almost eleven years old, I couldn't remember how. So, instead, I traded places with him and I held my mother on the kitchen chair as he desperately dialed for the help we needed.

In a moment everything had changed.

I had just been playing outside with my friend, Natalie, from my fifth grade class at school. We were off school that day because it was Good Friday. I asked my Mom if I could have a friend over, and though many of my friends had other plans, Natalie was available and we picked her up at her house earlier that afternoon. My brother, Nate, invited one of his second grade classmates, Tanner, over as well. The four of us planned to watch the movie *The Man from Snowy River* that evening after we jumped rope and rode bikes in the driveway.

"Do you think I need a jacket?" I asked my Mom as I neared the kitchen door that exited into the garage. She paused for a moment, then said that it was a little chilly and maybe I would want one. I ran back to my room and grabbed a jacket before hurrying out the door, with the screen door slamming behind me.

It was the last conversation I'd ever have with my mother.

My dad came outside and called us in to watch the movie. He left my mom sitting at the kitchen table, reading a book and sipping a cup of coffee. When we walked into the kitchen she was directly in front of us, slouching and falling off the chair.

What was wrong with her? Why was she limp and not responding to us? I held her upright in the chair and my own heart pounded in my chest. I felt cold and dizzy. Could she hear me telling her how much I loved her and that I thought everything was going to be okay? I was planning in my head what I would tell her later, how much she had scared me.

My dad hung up the phone and told us kids to go into the family room behind the kitchen. We did. He carried Mom to the front living room and laid her on the floor. He came back and pulled shut the flimsy accordion curtain door that hung between the family room and kitchen in an effort to shield our eyes and ears. And though it did protect us a little, it wasn't a steel curtain.

We sat stunned. Someone put the movie into the VCR and pushed play. The opening credits began to roll.

Tanner suggested that maybe we should pray. We did. *The Man from Snowy River* was well underway.

Finally, we heard the sirens of an ambulance as it pulled into our driveway.

The sounds of that night changed my life forever. To this day, the cry of the siren reaches to my soul and shakes me.

I can hear the murmurs of neighbors who had gathered in the dusk to watch the tragedy unfold.

The slam of police car doors closed me in as my dad, brother, and I followed the ambulance to the hospital, each of us shocked.

The silence echoes in the awful little room where we sat and waited for news. The small, sterile room soon held neighbors and a close friend, Dave Rahn, who sat beside us.

The doctor's words that filled the room and told us the news…

news that shakes me to the core even today.

"I'm sorry. We couldn't save her."

I can hear my thoughts as they flew through my head and swirled in confusion and painful, piercing shards of realization.

I can hear the crying of those who had gathered.

My grandma wailing as she walked onto the front porch of our home a few hours later.

My grandpa weeping as he began to speak of funeral plans.

My dad talking through his sobs as he called family members with the life-altering news: my mother had died suddenly, at the age of thirty-four, from a heart arrhythmia. The rheumatic fever she had suffered as a first grader weakened her heart more than anyone knew.

My heart was now damaged as well.

One final sound reminds me of her—the lid *pop*ping off the plastic tub as I look through her things. I love to look at the pictures, flip through her Bible and open her purse. I am always struck by the uncertainty of life when I look at her day planner and see appointments scheduled on the calendar, in her own handwriting, on dates she would not live to see.

It helps my heart to remember her.

My life has been changed forever because of all that I heard and saw on March 24, 1989.

But as difficult and painful as it is to remember, I don't want to forget.

*   *   *

The line at my mother's viewing stretched through the formal funeral home reception room and snaked against the wall all the way to the door. Most everyone wore downcast faces. Though their shoulders slumped and their faces pointed toward the ground, their eyes focused on us, my family, to see how we were responding to this tragedy.

I stood in front of Mom's open casket with my dad by my side. Other family members stood to our left and our right, flanked by lovely smelling floral arrangements whose brightness clashed with the dreary scene.

As I looked at Mom's body lying there so still and stiff, my own body ached. She still looked like herself. The dress she wore was one of her favorites. Her face portrayed a gentle and pleasant countenance, which was true to her sweet nature. Her hair was nicely styled. Her familiar hands lay crossed near her chest.

Yet a foreignness cloaked her figure. She looked wrong. Of course she did. How could her body appear alive when it was void of life? How could her temporary shell pass the inspection of a daughter who knew too well that this was not really her mom? Even so, I studied her, cramming my mind with everything I feared forgetting.

Those in attendance that day, as well as those who read about our loss in the newspaper, pitied the poor man who was now left to rear two young children on his own. What a tragedy for a young mother to die so suddenly.

Some people at the viewing tried to soothe our pain with gifts and words. I was given a flat and crunchy chocolate cookie in the shape of a teddy bear. White icing lined his features and I can still remember what he tasted like in my mouth, a little bitterness mixed with the sweet.

One woman stood in front of us and said, "God must have needed another alto in His angel choir!"

I cringed and then shook my head. "No, I don't think so," I responded. "The Bible doesn't ever say that people become angels when they die. Angels and people are two separate created beings." The woman's eyes grew large and her mouth closed slowly as she walked away. Though perhaps not the best time for a theological conversation, I could not let it pass. I had lost my mother, and trite comments about God needing another angel tasted more bitter and dry than the bear cookie.

Despite my youth, I did not wish to be talked down to or excluded. I wanted to face my reality head on and deal with it in my own way. That is why, later that day, after being taken to a friend's house for a break, I requested to be driven back to the funeral home. I had tried to allow myself to be distracted at Jennifer's house by watching *Anne of Green Gables*, but even the beloved character on the screen couldn't keep my attention. I wanted to be with my parents. Jennifer's mom understood and drove me back to the viewing.

As hard as it was for me to be there, I did not want to be anywhere else.

*   *   *

The fellowship hall of the church had never exuded warmth to me, but that spring day, the atmosphere chilled my heart. Long tables held a meal prepared for those of us who had just returned from the cemetery. Sandwiches made with deli ham took a prominent place. There was other food as well, but I don't remember what it was, and have, therefore, excused it much like a president pardons a Thanksgiving turkey. Deli ham, however, became a food forever tainted by my memory, much like contracting the stomach flu after eating a large wedge of watermelon. The watermelon wasn't the culprit, and although you know this deep down, you can't bring yourself to eat it for awhile. Why put the taste of that memory back into your mouth?

And, oh, the bitter taste that day held!

I had sat in a pew beside my dad as my mother lay lifeless in a coffin at the altar. Dr. Howard Cherry, for whom my mom had worked at the college, shared a eulogy. The voices of those in attendance stoically and robotically echoed the chorus to "It Is Well."

As we sang the hymn, "Great Is Thy Faithfulness," my face dripped with tears and my voice stuck in my throat. At the phrase, "strength for today and bright hope for tomorrow," I crumbled. I laid my head on my dad's shoulder and continued to weep.

Strength for today. I desperately needed it.

Strength to get me through that verse, that song, that service. Strength to move my body, wearing a dress my mom had helped me pick at the store, down the aisle. Strength to walk out the front doors of the church with my dad and my brother behind the coffin of our fourth family member. It would be the last time the four of us would ever be together physically. My grandma told me later what a poignant and awful sight it was, the finality of it made clear by the hearse waiting at the curb. Strength to leave my mother's body at a cemetery where it would stay and never again come home with us.

And hope for tomorrow? Tomorrow seemed very far away.

My yesterdays had been charmed. I had lived a happy childhood with two loving parents and a fun friend of a brother.

I don't believe I took my wonderful childhood for granted. The night my mom died, I sat in my living room after returning from the hospital. Across from me, in the wingback chair, was a family friend whom my dad had called to be with us while we waited for extended family to arrive. My eyes met Dave's and I said, "At least we can be thankful for the time we had with her." And I meant it. I knew I had been blessed.

My yesterdays had been good.

But hope for tomorrow?

As I collapsed against my dad's shoulder at the funeral I was resting upon his physical presence. But, as the years would go by, I would rest more on his words. On something he had said the night my mom had died.

We stood in a sterile hospital room. Not a room with a bed and TV, but a room with a hard metal table. My dad, even in the deepest grief of his life, had the wisdom to ask the doctor if we could see our mom's body, and so now we stood around her. Though it may sound morbid or scary, it was actually just the opposite.

It was helpful.

My dad, Nate, and I were able to say good-bye to Mom and give her one last kiss. Dad then reminded us that what we saw was just my mom's body and not really Mom. We held hands and prayed together, and my dad told us that even though we were heartbroken and we didn't understand this, he believed God was still in control.

Dad offered me hope for tomorrow. In the days and years to follow, I would cling to it.

His words resonated and affirmed all that I had learned while paying attention in Sunday school since I was a tiny child wearing Mary Janes and sitting on the cold, hard folding chair in the church basement. Now, as Dad guided me through these important truths, I was able to trust them and take them to heart because they were consistent with how we'd lived and what I'd learned for as long as I could remember.

By pointing me to a God who was unchanging in a moment when my entire world had just been completely thrown off its axis, my dad gave me hope that God could not only handle the change, but would remain in control of it.

By reminding me that God is sovereign and good in a moment where everything seemed so utterly unfair, my dad gave me hope that I could trust that God not only knew about my mom's death, but that He cared about us and loved us even in our pain. In fact, He was grieving too.

By leading me in prayer around the bed where my dead mother lay, my dad reminded me that I could always turn to my Heavenly Father for comfort, hope, and love.

My six-year-old brother would later say that though the day my mom died was called Good Friday, it wasn't a very good day for us. So very true.

But, because of the death of another, Jesus, on that first Good Friday many yesterdays ago, I have hope for tomorrow.

Thirteen years after my mom's death I would once again lean on my dad's shoulder as we sang the song "Great Is Thy Faithfulness" in a church. Dad had just walked me down the aisle, and before giving me away, we stood and sang as a congregation. Instead of looking at a coffin, I was looking at the smiling face of the man I was thrilled to marry. I had chosen that same hymn and, though I was too choked up for my voice to be audible, I mouthed the words and smiled as we sang the phrase, "Strength for today and bright hope for tomorrow," because my tomorrow had arrived.

But you can be sure we didn't serve ham at the reception.

*   *   *

I was hesitant to return to school after the death of my mother. Fifth grade classrooms aren't known for empathy and tenderness, but about a week after the funeral, I did return.

I didn't stay for long.

My life had started to change even before I lost my mother on March 24. The transitions only became more drastic the further we moved through 1989.

In January, my dad, who had been working for the denominational headquarters of The Church of the United Brethren in Christ, had taken a new job as the pastor of a small church in Fort Wayne, Indiana. Though just about sixteen miles down the highway, the church was in a different community, and, therefore, a different school system. My parents had decided that we should move closer to the church and had begun building a house in the one-traffic-light town of Roanoke.

We could move closer to Emmanuel, our new church, yet stay in our current school system. We would eventually attend the same high school where we'd been planning to attend all along, but we would need to change elementary schools after we moved. My parents thought this was the best scenario and compromise. They couldn't have known what was to come, and I do not fault them for this decision, though it turned out to be a rough one. It meant I would face a new classroom of fifth graders, this time all strangers, just weeks after the worst experience of my life.

I also had a new social sphere at church. The kids with whom I'd attended Vacation Bible School, Wednesday evening programming, and Sunday school for the previous two years, after our move to Indiana, remained in Huntington.

Emmanuel Community Church averaged about seventy people in attendance on Sunday mornings. The tiny brick building sat on a hill amongst many trees with a gravel driveway leading up to the gravel lot. Many weeks, my Sunday school class consisted of the teacher, me, and one or two other boys my age. We met in a small room with red carpet behind the sanctuary. The entrance of the tiny church building did not include pillars.

Six weeks after my dad took the pastorate at Emmanuel, my mom died. Just weeks after the funeral, our new house was complete. Our new family of three moved to a new house in a new town where we were sent to a new school Monday through Friday while attending a new church on Sunday.

Much like years before, when I had laid in a hospital bed with my right arm in traction and my desired thumb out of reach, now many comforts and securities had been ripped from me once again.

The book had closed on life as I knew it, and now a blank book was lying open in front of me.

Change was the intended plotline. I'm not a fan of that genre.

I approach change much like a cat being pulled by a toddler toward a mud puddle. I dig my heels deep into the ground and sometimes snarl. But 1989 had a tight grip on me and had been dragging me through the mud, indeed. I was sad, but I did not put up much of a fight. I was pretty sure it would only drain my energy and would otherwise make little difference.

With so much being out of my control, I needed to control something, and that something was my own attitude. Much like the first grade version of myself with the broken arm, I was determined to be mature and handle things well. At the age of eleven I was on the brink of becoming a young lady, but was still a child. I saw things plainly as they really were, yet my young eyes cast a naïve and innocent hue on the darkest moments. I worked hard to be strong for my dad, and for Nate, and for the masses who now looked on our family with pity.

I tried to find the light within the darkness. And as is often the case, I noticed things as a child that sometimes grown-ups don't.

Things like the snow globe my fifth grade class in Huntington presented to me before I moved away. On its pink plastic base stood a little blonde girl with a white butterfly net. Her watery world had to be shaken in order to help the free-floating butterflies to fall into her net, but then they'd slowly settle as the world around her became still once again. It read across the front, "May Only Good Things Come Your Way."

There was the friend who came to my house the weekend after my mother died armed with a box of tissues and ears to listen as we sat on my bed and I told her, "I just can't believe it."

The ladies from Emmanuel, our new church, took me under their wings and loved me as if I was their own daughter. At a time when I physically ached whenever friends talked about going to the grocery store with their moms, those women included me in their lives. Betty, Susie, and Gia took me to the mall to go bathing suit shopping. I smiled much of the day and enjoyed a moment of normal, a pre-teen girl at the mall with other women.

Another woman from Emmanuel, Margo, let me hang out at her house often. She also opened her heart to me. She allowed me to talk about and process the changes in my life, while at the same time making me smile and laugh in the present.

And Joan, who lived back in Pennsylvania, and who had been my Sunday school teacher when I just a little girl in pigtailed braids, sent me letters in the mail. Joan never missed a birthday or holiday, and her neat and pretty handwriting filled page after page. She made me feel as if I was not forgotten. And when I wrote back to her, she'd respond, which made me feel as if what I had to say was important.

Friends helped us move into our new home. Peeling manufacturer's stickers off of the double sinks in the upstairs bathroom reminded me again that even the most mundane parts of my life were brand new.

A kind teacher in my new classroom at Roanoke Elementary helped me set up my desk so that I would feel more at home.

My dad, through his own grief, did his very best to carry on with life. I could see the burden on his shoulders, sometimes almost literally, as he drove our minivan with his forearms laid on top of the steering wheel as if it was too difficult to sit up fully. I worried about him.

He had tried to resign as pastor of Emmanuel, thinking that he no longer could preach and lead. But though he turned in his resignation several times, the church leaders wouldn't accept it during this time of grief. Instead they encouraged him to stay. He returned to the pulpit weeks after his wife's death. Each week before the service he'd lay face down on his office floor in tears trying to muster up the strength to bring the Word of God to others. He first needed to minister to his own heart.

The first few months of 1989 were full of changes. And I was changed by each one. But I had learned years earlier, when I had broken my right arm, that just because something is not ideal doesn't mean it is not okay.

This was affirmed years later on December 7, 2002. On the night of our wedding, my husband and I were given a card in which my dad had written, in beautiful cursive script, a message to my brand new husband. It read that, other than me being a little too emotional at times and not handling change well, he thought Kraig was marrying a near "perfect ten." There it was, on paper, my aversion to change... and in a congratulatory wedding card to my new husband, no less. But reading between those cursive lines I could see more than my weaknesses being spelled out in ink. I could see that my dad was proud of who I had become. The changes of 1989 hadn't simply closed the book on a season of our lives, but had turned the page to many new chapters. Chapters full of hope, joy, and brand new love.

life morsel: When change rocks your world, when death stings, live anyway. God offers strength and hope for the living.

Top: This family picture was taken just months before my mom passed away

Right: At my mother's gravesite as a young adult. In this photo I was about the age she was when she passed away

three

cereal for supper

why we ate it so often and how we finally kicked the habit

He bent over the bed to kiss me goodnight. I was thankful for his presence in my life. I had dealt with the fear that after losing my mom I would lose Dad, too.

One night the fear had overwhelmed me and I was just sure that, as I lay in my bedroom trying to sleep, something awful had happened to him out in the family room. I mustered the strength to leave my bed and check on him but I found him merely sitting on the couch.

"What's wrong?" he asked.

"I don't know. I just thought maybe something bad happened to you." Feeling a little embarrassed, I wanted to hide under my covers.

"Did you sense something bad was going to happen to Mom before it did?"

I thought about it for a moment. "No."

I guess logic often gives way to fear, especially in the mind of an eleven-year-old. But over time, this improved.

Being bitten in the eye by the neighbor's dog had made me fearful of dogs initially, but though a scar reminds me that some dogs do bite, one mean dog won't keep me away from all other canines in my life. After my mom died, I dealt with the fear that death would take other loved ones. As the wound healed, granted more slowly than the one over my eye had, my fear of another loss diminished as well, though never leaving completely. The loss of my mother will not keep me from opening my heart to others.

That would be allowing death to win, and I choose to give life a fighting chance.

A few months later as Dad was tucking me in, I worried less about losing him and instead thought more often about the idea of gaining someone else.

I thought we needed a new woman in our lives.

I said as much to my dad that night. I expressed that though we were "making it" all right, I really thought Nate and I could use a new mom. Someone to care for us as only a mom can. Someone to feed us something for supper other than cold cereal, though Dad had done quite well putting it on the table.

"Well, that's interesting," Dad said. "You'll have to think about what qualities you'd want in that woman," he added in an effort to divert the conversation and escape from both the room and the topic.

"Oh, I already have," I responded as I reached over and pulled a piece of paper out of my Bible.

On it I had listed the qualities I'd like in a new mom.

Dad took the list out of my hand and read the first item.

1. She can swim.

Clearly I had put some serious thought into this.

"She can swim?" Dad asked with raised eyebrows.

My mom, Mary, had not been able to swim and feared the water. Though she desperately wanted to splash around with Nate and me, her fear prevented it. I had struggled with this and had really wanted her to swim with us. Swimming with us kids represented being "all in."

Don't misunderstand, my mom was most definitely "all in" about loving and parenting Nate and me, and I do not blame her for her fear. But if I was to be blessed with a new mom, I wanted her to swim. And I wanted a mom who would participate in activities with Nate and me. She should play in the backyard, be involved in what we were doing, and not solely sit on the sidelines.

I explained this to Dad and he nodded slowly. He looked over the rest of the list, which was much more along the traditional lines of wants in a new mother: nice, good with kids, can cook something other than frozen Banquet pot pies.

"Well, if you are serious about this then we'd better pray for this woman," Dad said as he handed back the list and began to leave the room.

I was serious all right. And I prayed.

I was ready for my dad to start dating. I never for a moment thought anyone could replace my mom. That would be simply impossible. But I had a lot of love in my heart, and I was ready to share it with someone new. And goodness knows we needed her.

We were tired of swimming alone.

*   *   *

Just three months after the death of my mother, my dad met someone. In my eyes, this was not too fast to start dating again. I had already considered what I'd wanted in a new mom and had given Dad my permission to date. He said he was not ready, nor interested, but that was beside the point.

Nevertheless, it happened.

At the June wedding of a family friend, for which we traveled back to Pennsylvania, my dad was introduced to a single lady from Detroit, Michigan. She happened to be the groom's aunt and the sister of my dad's close friend. There was some conniving and arm twisting, and maybe a few white lies told by family members to basically force the two of them to have coffee after the reception, but no matter whose side of the story I hear recounted now, the ending is the same. Dennis Miller and Karin Newman began a long-distance dating relationship and a short-lived engagement. They were married on October 7, 1989.

Thus, 1989 continued to be the year of change.

As my dad dated Karin, I was blissfully unaware of proper widower dating etiquette, of how fast the changes appeared to outsiders. I liken my mindset during those days to the way I once felt when our neighbors rang our doorbell one evening and asked if they could go down to our basement because of a tornado warning. My family was sitting around the kitchen table eating dinner and we happily welcomed our neighbors in and showed them the basement door. Then we finished our meal at the table. I found it slightly perplexing that our neighbors saw reason to be in our basement, yet we did not. But, I followed my parents' lead. And I was hungry. So I stayed happily in my seat. Ignorance is bliss, and sometimes it causes those around you to question your sanity. It didn't matter. Dad's relationship with Karin thrilled me!

Karin was a thirty-nine-year-old businesswoman. She had worked her way up in the grocery business at A&P, now working in their corporate offices. She had never been married, had no children, and had very little baggage of the literal or figurative kind. She was kind and came from a great family, some of whom we knew from Pennsylvania. In fact, her nieces had been my babysitters when I was little.

The Newman family had my approval, and though we didn't know Karin Newman until after my mom's death, I now liked her as well. We all did.

Dad and Karin would meet each other for meals part way between Fort Wayne and Detroit. Sometimes she'd visit at our house and a few times we went to visit her at her condo.

And much to my delight, I learned that Karin could swim. The first time we swam at a pool, she joined us in the water. My prayers had been answered. Priority number one could be checked off the list.

My dad proposed and the wedding plans began. I went dress shopping with Karin, tickled to be allowed to wear high heels in the wedding, though I was nervous I wouldn't be able to walk well. I practiced at home. Steady and slow.

This was going to be an important trip down the aisle, toward once again becoming a family of four.

*   *   *

I sat in the front pew of the church as the wedding reception wound down in the nearby Fellowship Hall. I was crying. Why did they have to leave on a honeymoon? I was ready to start being a family now. How unfair that they could leave for a week without Nate and me!

Once again one of the women from church, who had so faithfully cared for and loved me during that time, gently sat beside me and told me that it was important for me to let them go.

"They'll be back soon, and this time is important for them," Margo said. "You'll enjoy the week with your grandparents and your aunt and uncle. Come on, stop crying. It's going to be okay."

And she was right. It was okay.

For the most part, as 1989 drew to a close, life started to feel almost normal again.

I was in sixth grade, which was my final year of elementary school. I had a teacher whom I loved, and I had made many new friends in Roanoke.

Dad and Karin decided to build a house across town so that we wouldn't have the visual reminders each day of the house and life he and

49

my mom had built together. Once again we were transitioning. At least this time I did not have to change schools or churches. The new house may have been on the other side of Roanoke, but that was less than two miles away.

There were moments when I felt the ache of all of the changes in my life. Sometimes I'd sit and just think in order to process it all. Sometimes I'd write in my journal. And sometimes I'd talk to a trusted adult.

One day at school in sixth grade my teacher called me out into the hall. I knew I wasn't in trouble, so I didn't understand why she'd singled me out. As I leaned against the cold lockers, she asked me if I was okay. "Is something wrong, Christy?"

"I don't know," I responded. "I just am struggling with something."

"Do you want to talk about it?"

I took some deep breaths and then through teary eyes told her that I felt confused and stuck. I loved Karin, and really liked her as well. I was happy that Dad had married her, but I wanted to talk about my mom. I was afraid doing so would hurt Karin's feelings.

All but one of our family photos had been put away on the closet shelf. All memories and conversations of my mom seemed stuffed away as well. I didn't like that, and I didn't want that, but Karin's heart mattered, too.

My teacher sweetly told me that she could see my dilemma. She also told me that she thought Karin would understand and that I should tell her my feelings.

Later in the year, when a classmate's mother died from cancer, I found myself in the school guidance counselor's office. I hadn't chosen to go there, but was summoned along with the grieving boy from my class so that we could sit together with the counselor and share our feelings on this shared loss. I sat in my chair and looked at him. He sat in his chair and looked at me.

"I'm sorry," I said.

"I'm sorry too," he said. Then we looked back at the counselor. We weren't sure what else we were supposed to say. But since I was with the guidance counselor, I once again brought up my concerns. The counselor told me that I could and should talk about my mom. Karin would understand.

Karin had left a life in the business world instantly to become a pastor's wife and mother of two. Her life had been turned upside down, as well as ours, and though she was thrilled and loved us greatly, it was still a transition. I didn't want to add to her difficulty by bringing up the woman who had loved us and given birth to the children for whom Karin now cared.

But, over time I did tell Karin about this struggle, and she was more gracious than I thought possible. She told me that I could talk about my mom anytime, and that I could talk to her about it, or if I preferred to talk to my dad alone, that was fine, too. She never made the subject of my mom taboo, and any pressure not to talk about Mom was only self-inflicted.

I am grateful to this day for Karin's understanding and for the unselfish love she shows my dad, Nate, and me. Karin almost never promotes herself, but serves others constantly. She is my stepmother, but she defies the stereotypical imagery associated with step-parenting. Perhaps that is why several weeks after the wedding I chose to call her "Mom." It was a conscience decision, and one I didn't take lightly. I knew that this didn't diminish or replace my first mom, but, instead, this claimed the fact that I'd been blessed by two amazing moms.

I'll never forget walking up the steps to my dad and Karin's bedroom one day with a piece of paper in hand. I don't recall the contents of the paper, but I wanted to show it to Karin and I used it as an excuse to call her name. It was the name by which I would address her from that day forward.

"Hey, Mom, I want to show you something!"

*   *   *

I've heard it said that if you hear hoof beats behind you, expect horses, not zebras. The phrase means to expect the most common and natural circumstances, which are most likely what will come to pass, not something rare or absurd.

As a young child I only envisioned horses behind me. Actually, it is probably fairer to say that I never considered anything looming in my future at all. However, as a preteen, who had now experienced a very tumultuous "zebra" or two in her life, I did begin to expect the unexpected. Difficult circumstances no longer surprised me when they approached and then left me in a cloud of dust.

One such example occurred less than a year after my dad remarried. In July of 1990, Mom (Karin) was involved in a car accident. She was injured, but stable. I was babysitting at the time and was not immediately taken to the hospital to see her when I learned of the crash. I was angry and frustrated. In fact, the next day I wrote this in my diary.

July 29, 1990

"Well diary,
I guess it's been ages since I've written. Looking back at the last entry I seemed so happy. Today I am not one bit happy. It takes a lot to smile, my eyes are tired and I wish I could scream my

lungs out. *The reason for all this is, my mom was in a car accident yesterday, and not just a little one. A drunk driver hit the car in front of my mom and sent Mom over the road. Mom went down in a ditch (a very deep one) and hit a bunch of trees. The van was totaled (we think) and Mom's right arm was totally crushed. But Mom is home across the hall in her room sleeping. She has a cast on her right arm that goes all the way up to her shoulder (yuck) and it's heavy too. She's going to need a lot of help. Because of this we probably won't be able to go on vacation to Pennsylvania, North Carolina, and Mom and Dad were going to go to Israel but now we might not be able to go anywhere and that makes me very mad. I was looking forward to all of them very, very much. Well, off this bad news and I'll tell you some good news. Well, the last entry, June 19, says about softball and winning two games and losing one. Well, it's been so long since I've written that softball season is over! And guess what?! Our team, the Turpins, was #1! We won the first place title. We didn't get trophies, but we did get necklaces or medallions that are gold for first place. Crestwood team got silver for second and Whistlestop got bronze for third. It was great. Well, I'll keep you posted on Mom and how bad the van is."*

Christy

Another zebra had run into my life. This one did not take the life of my mom and the pain it brought was more temporary. For that I was grateful.

And, apparently, winning a gold medallion in softball was a pretty good distraction.

life morsel: Sometimes loss offers us unexpected blessings.

Top: Becoming a new family of four October 7, 1989

Below: The Miller family. Here I was in high school and Nate in middle school

four

gatorade and daily bread

why they remind me of important life lessons

Softball was not the only sport that became a positive distraction in my preteen years. I played basketball starting in sixth grade.

I use the words "played" and "basketball" loosely here. I really had no clue what was going on. I don't remember ever attending a basketball game prior to playing in one.

If that wasn't enough, I suffered an injury (not related to basketball but due to a person related to me—in the form of a brother) and was eventually out for the season.

It was quite a year.

I was a Stonewall, though. A Roanoke Elementary School Stonewall named in honor of Andrew "Stonewall" Jackson.

We sixth graders were given a chance to play basketball in hopes of preparing us for our upcoming entrance into the big time world of middle school sports.

Goodness knows I needed the preparation.

I sat on the bench beside my gangly teammates, watching as five girls from my team flailed up and down the court with five opponents. The gym was jammed with high socks, big bangs, and minimal skill.

My coach strode to the bench and told me that I would sub in for one of the other girls.

"*Cool*," I thought. I rose and ran in

Apparently, such eagerness is frowned upon.

Protocol required I check in at the scorer's table and then wait for a time-out or dead ball when they would "buzz me in" to the game. News to me.

The basket seemed so high and the dribbling so difficult. Yet, I did gain some game experience under my elastic waistband.

But then my brother body-slammed me in our basement (that's another story having to do not with a stone wall, but a concrete floor) and effectively ended my season.

But all was not lost. My sympathetic teammates designed a t-shirt for me at the mall. It was white with an orange airbrushed basketball wearing sunglasses on the front. They even airbrushed my first name in bubble letters across the back.

With perks like this, maybe basketball belonged in my future.

*　　*　　*

My parents noticed my increasing interest in sports as I continued into the ever-awkward middle school years. They wanted to foster what little skill I had at that point to help me discover if basketball was truly where I wanted to put my future time and effort. So, Mom and Dad presented me with a gift on Christmas morning. But unlike the airbrushed t-shirt, this gift left us all feeling a little deflated.

When I began tearing off the pretty paper, I pried and pulled at the cardboard flaps, trying to lift open the top of the plain brown box, but I couldn't break past the layer of stubborn tape. So I'd done what any half-brained teenager (with no desire to fetch a pair of scissors) would do. I asked my grandpa for his pocketknife.

Just call me MacGyver.

Except MacGyver would have known better.

Instead of sliding the blade along the taped seal, I jabbed the knife full force into the lid. Effective for butchering a 10-point buck out on the back forty, but slight overkill for Christmas morning in the family room.

But I butchered something, all right. My gift.

As I sheepishly pulled the deflating basketball out of the now open box, my parents deflated as well. They quickly moved through the stages of gift-giving grief: shock, to denial, to disappointment, to utter confusion.

Commentary sprang from the whole gang: my parents, brother, and grandparents.

"Why did you jab it? Why didn't you just cut the tape like a normal person?"

"Do you hear it hissing? Oh, my, it's going to be totally flat!"

"You won't even be able to take it back to the store now."

I had no response, at least not a good one. I didn't know why I had opened the gift as if it was something vicious needing to be put down. But what was done, was done.

I tenderly folded the little knife back up into its plastic home and gingerly handed it back to my grandpa. The ball finished hissing and now lay in a sad rubbery heap on my lap. Everyone sat quietly. Perhaps an unscripted moment of silence for the ball that was lost.

My dad, who sometimes kicks into a "let's make lemonade out of these lemons" mode, had one last thing to say.

"Well, at least it wasn't a puppy."

*   *   *

When I wasn't destroying basketballs, I was learning to dribble and shoot one. Basketball became a big part of my life in middle school, and especially in the summers following.

I played on the Junior Lady Vikings (AAU) basketball team with girls from Huntington County. Our schedule included between sixty and seventy games each summer.

And I learned a great deal. Not only did I learn how to execute a better layup and play better defense, I found that principles learned on the court carried over to "real life" as well.

Be a team player. Life is not all about you. Nobody likes a bragger.

If you want to be good at something, you must put effort into it, even if you have natural talent. And especially if you don't. I am not naturally athletic. In fact, I had to work harder than the majority of the girls on my team to learn even the basic skills. But I learned that often, over time, determination and hard work pass raw talent, or at least catch up to it.

Friends do not need to look or act like you. In fact, you may have very different lives, play different positions, and bring different strengths to the team. This is very good. Differences are not hindrances, but assets. Envy and comparison stop you short. Love and kindness go a long way.

If a coach throws a clipboard, get out of the way.

I learned that Gatorade upsets my stomach. Water quenches my thirst. In fact, I love water. I drink water all day long, even now when I'm rarely defending anyone or running drills. Water has become a daily habit for me that both refreshes and purifies. I don't need the added flavors and electrolytes. Water is enough.

I have very weak hands. But much like my college GPA, I've learned this doesn't really matter later in life.

Nonverbal communication is sometimes more effective than words. My freshman year, I played on the junior varsity team instead of the freshman team, mostly due to my experience playing AAU the prior two summers. I was a decent player, but no prodigy. However, I allowed my head to swell and began to think I was "too good" to play on the freshman team with my peers. One week, the JV team did not have a scheduled game and Coach asked me to play with the freshmen. During a timeout, the coach instructed the girls in the huddle. I felt as if I didn't need to hear those instructions. I stood several feet away, waiting for my teammates to catch up to my level of preparedness. Then, as I tipped my head back to drink from my water bottle, proudly standing outside the huddle, I caught my dad's eye as he sat in the bleachers. With one glance, I "heard" all I needed to hear. It was a silent, but powerful sermon. My pride and arrogance glared me in the eyes. And they were ugly. Thankfully, I was humiliated. I walked over to the huddle and listened.

In basketball and in life, it is important to have your head in the game.

Sometimes burdens turn out to be blessings. Breaking my right arm in first grade turned out to be good training. Adapting to using my left hand for daily tasks had paid off as now I easily learned to shoot and dribble with my left hand. It turns out a silver lining does exist, even inside plaster casts.

Offense wins games. Defense wins championships. It's about more than scoring points.

Seasons change, in basketball and in life. My sophomore year of high school I played junior varsity again and a little varsity. We had great talent in our midst. One of our teammates was later given the coveted title of "Indiana Miss Basketball." The team played very well that year and the following year went on to win the state championship. However, I had quit the team. Basketball was ruling my life. My coach frowned upon involvement in other extracurricular activities and even other school sports. I had played volleyball, and I wished to attend church youth group and other social activities. I also wanted to try out for a school musical and put more time into my Advanced Art class projects. As a teenager, I lacked perspective about time. I did not understand that there are seasons and rhythm to life. A few months of full-time commitment was just a drop in the bucket of living. I didn't understand that these opportunities possessed a "limited time offer." So with a good heart and intentions to balance my life, I quit basketball mid-season my sophomore year.

"If the ball would have rolled your way more often, would you still be quitting?" my coach asked as I stood in the hall handing him my uniform. "Yes," I said. "It's not about how I am playing or how much. I need room for some other things." He shook his head and took my things before turning and walking back into the gym.

I look back on that decision now with a bit of regret. Though I applaud my own effort to keep life in proper perspective and to prioritize the things I deemed most important, I know now that maybe I could have done that while also being committed to basketball.

You live, and you learn, and hopefully you apply what you have learned to the next situation. Now when I feel overwhelmed with the season of life I am in, and my schedule feels full and daunting, I keep this in mind. As King Solomon said in Ecclesiastes 3, "There is a time for everything, and a season for every activity under the heavens." I doubt he was referring to basketball, but I get his point.

Life is full of seasons. We can choose to learn from and enjoy each one, even if they are not ideal.

I am thankful for the season of basketball in my own life. I learned a great deal. And when I did quit basketball, I was able to go on to play Mrs. Doris MacAfee in our high school's production of *Bye, Bye, Birdie* my senior year. I also did well enough in art class to earn a small art scholarship for college (which I subsequently lost after changing my major from graphic design to ministry).

Sometimes you win, and sometimes you lose.

But it sure is a gift to be given the chance to play the game.

*   *   *

Excerpt from my Basketball Goals journal, 1991-1992 (eighth grade)

Short Term Goals:
- *Improve on offensive moves under the basket*
- *Learn to anticipate offensively and defensively on the court*
- *Come to meet passes*
- *Square-up when shooting, and take a good shot. Hold my follow-through and put a lot of arch on the ball*
- *Front the person I'm guarding and be a good weak-side helper*
- *Improve on free throws. Use my legs, arch, follow-through straight*
- *Be a good encourager to my Junior Lady Vikings team*
- *Don't anger easily. Keep control of yourself and your head up, even if you have four fouls*
- *JLV- beat Anderson "Lady Netters" April 18, 1992*
- *Win Heritage Days and White River tournaments*
- *Keep a good attitude in winning and in losing*

Mid-term Goals:
- *Make the freshman and Junior Varsity team in Freshman year*
- *Start on Junior Varsity team Sophomore year, maybe play a little Varsity*
- *Play Varsity and be starting by the end of Junior year*
- *Start Varsity Senior Year*

- *Win a State Championship my Junior and possibly Senior year*

Long-Term Goals:
- *Scholarships for basketball*
- *NAIA basketball championship*
- *Basketball coach someday*

*   *   *

My two-door, white Dodge Neon, with its cute spoiler and fun round headlights, made me smile. It was the first car I had purchased on my own. That is, if "on my own" can be expanded to include the nice people at the bank who loaned me money and had given me a little blue payment book. Each month, I took the Neon through the bank drive-thru and put my payment book and a check into the tube that rode through the tunnel to the friendly teller.

My Neon was just as friendly. In fact, I always claimed that it just exuberated the word "Hi" to its fellow four-wheeled comrades as I drove it down the road. My family raised their eyebrows but associated with me anyway.

Imagine my surprise when a few months later, Dodge aired a commercial where the Dodge Neon was shown driving down the road with the word "Hi" above it.

It was my idea first and though this justified my sanity to my family, Dodge never compensated me for the rights to the idea. Maybe the check is still lost in the mail.

It was in my Neon that I learned a good lesson about bread. Daily bread.

I was in the driver's seat and my dad was riding shotgun. As usual, I had a CD of Christian music playing. This one was a compilation of 1996's greatest hits.

"I really like these lyrics," I told Dad. "I want to trust God like this, too."

Bryan Duncan's tenor voice continued to drift through the speakers as he sang about how he wished to surrender his tomorrows to God. He melodically promised he would give God control over each and every day to come.

Dad wasn't quite as impressed.

"I understand what he's saying," Dad said, "but I don't think you can really do that."

I made my scrunchy "Are you serious?" face and looked at Dad out of the corner of my eye.

"What do you mean? He's saying that he is giving God every day of his future. He's trusting God with tomorrow and the next day and the next day . . ."

I repeated my reasoning several times but Dad clearly disagreed.

Finally, I paused for breath and Dad spoke up. "I think we can trust God in general with our future, but we can't just say we give God every day and be done with it. We have to give God each day, each hour, each moment. We can't just trust Him with our future once and never think about it again. We tend to take back our trust and then worry and fear. So, I get his point, but I think trust is a daily thing."

Being a pastor's kid is sometimes a drag.

But you know what? That CD of 1996's greatest hits is collecting dust somewhere, and Bryan Duncan is no spring chicken, yet I still haven't forgotten that conversation. Or the point.

Trust is a daily discipline. Much like basketball had been a daily physical discipline.

I've been reminded of this truth as I've grown older and more mature in my faith. I've seen places in both the Old and New Testament where it was taught. And I've been encouraged.

I hate to say it, but I think Dad was right.

Jesus Himself taught His disciples how to pray in the Lord's Prayer in Matthew 6 (KJV). It's a short and concise prayer, yet in one sentence He is purposely redundant when He says, " Give us this day our daily bread."

Jesus doesn't ask for bread for tomorrow, or the next day, or the day after the day after that...

He asks for bread for today.

Jesus knew that trusting God for our provision, whether physical or spiritual, was a daily exercise. We can't store it up and call it done for next week or next year.

In fact, if we try, it spoils. It grows mold.

The shelf life of trust is short.

How do I know this? I look at the Israelites who were led in the wilderness for forty years waiting to enter the Promised Land. God fed them with a daily bread called Manna. Exodus 16: 4 says, "Then the Lord said to Moses, 'I will rain down bread from heaven for you. The people are to go out each day and gather enough for that day. In this way I will test them and see whether they will follow my instructions.'"

The people could only take enough provision for that day. Daily bread.

Now some of the Israelites must have heard Bryan Duncan's song and thought that they could store some bread up for the next day so they gathered a bit more than today's portion. It didn't go well for them.

Exodus 16: 19-20 tell us, "Then Moses said to them, 'No one is to keep any of it until morning.' However, some of them paid no attention to

Moses; they kept part of it until morning, but it was full of maggots and began to smell."

So maybe mold was an understatement. We're talking maggot farm here.

I think I'll pass on tomorrow's bread.

Manna and Jesus' prayer make it very clear to me that bread is to be a daily thing.

My trust in God, and God's provision, is for today.

I've been blessed with wonderful manna. God's provision is always enough for the day. It is always enough.

And I have stopped striving to be a bread and trust hoarder. I don't like worms. I'm happy to have my daily bread. It sustains me perfectly.

So, it turns out that little sermon I heard for free in my Neon made quite an impact in my thinking. I'm grateful for that.

Now let's just hope the check from Dodge will cover the court costs when Bryan Duncan reads this.

life morsel: Tomorrow's peace can't be bottled today. It won't stay fresh.

Right: In my middle school basketball uniform (note my stylish "poofy" hair!)

Below: At the dealership the day I bought my Dodge Neon, the car that just said "Hi!"
My grandfather, "Pappy" came along for the occasion

five

the dish

how I prepared to meet Mr. Right

I wasn't allowed to date until the age of sixteen, so I had plenty of time to prepare. Well, my appearance, anyway.

It's easy to picture the young teenage girl spending hours in front of the mirror readying for a date. She's applied her makeup just right. The masterpiece displayed in the form of her hair took hours to complete, but looks much like it does every other day. And her outfit, well, judging from the piles of rejected pants, skirts, and shirts on the bed and floor, this one outfit has been chosen as the ensemble supreme.

The preparation for the date is complete. Now she just needs a guy.

My sophomore year of high school, the year I turned sixteen, a few guys asked me out. I accepted, and even dated one of them for four months.

I continued to prepare for the dating season I'd now entered.

I curled my bangs, both over and under, hair spraying the resulting poof into near permanency.

I wore the right *Guess* jeans and sported my *Eastland* loafers with pride.

I enjoyed the company of the boys who took me out, and I sincerely had fun going to the mall, out to dinner, or on walks to the park.

But then I broke up with the boys.

Breaking up was a major part of the preparation for me, too.

You know those girls who date a lot of boys in high school and college as "research" to find out what they really like in a guy and what kind of man they want to marry?

I wasn't one of them.

Frankly, I already had a pretty good idea.

I'd even written it down.

In addition to Pantene and Dep hair gel, I'd also invested in writing a list of the qualities I wanted in a husband and then I asked God to bring that man into my life. I remembered that specifically and intentionally praying about qualities I wanted in a new mom had worked out quite well. Why not try the same technique for a potential husband?

Now before you think this was too rigid or bold let me explain that I had an "essential" and a "non-essential" column. I gave God plenty of room to work.

Turns out these types of requests take a while.

Though I had many guy friends in both high school and college, I dated very few. Some days, I greatly disliked the single season and wished for dates just for a confidence boost, if nothing more, but most days I was content. I somehow knew that it, or should I say he, would be worth the wait.

But at one point during my college years, my Grandma Miller decided she was tired of waiting and she gave me this unsolicited advice,

"Christy, I think you should cross a few things off that list of yours! Do you really think you're going to find a guy that matches all of those things?"

Thanks, Grandma.

But, yes, I did think he existed.

Surely there was a guy out there who matched my list items of being both taller than my 5' 8" and loving the Lord with all of his heart. There had to be a man alive who wanted a family, was good with children, worked in ministry, loved to sing, and sometimes wore glasses. I mean really, I wasn't asking for a Heisman winner or Nobel recipient.

And, so, I ignored my Grandma and waited.

While I waited, I graduated from Huntington University with an educational ministries and Bible degree, and I took a job at my local church as the Director of Children's Ministries.

I worked. I waited. And I prayed.

And it was a good thing I did.

*   *   *

Excerpt from journal dated December 12, 1996 (First semester of Freshman year of college)

Lord,

I want to write this prayer to you to show you how serious I am. Father, I really need your help. I need your strength and understanding and also your patience. I have a strong desire in my heart to get married and have a family.

Lord, as I sit here in the library, and have gone through my first four months of this semester, I have been keeping an eye out for "Mr. Perfect." I am in the habit of wondering if my future is going to be spent with just about every guy I pass on the way to class or see in the Dining Commons. Thoughts about my future have been consuming my daily thoughts. My hunger for marriage, and family serving together in ministry is growing every day. I need your patience, Lord, to wait for your timing. I know I won't ever understand your plan, but I promise I never want to be out of it.

I will serve as a single woman missionary in the jungles of Africa if that is your plan for me, Father. You know the desires of my heart and I trust that you will guide me along in

*your plan and you will either change my heart or surprise me
with something even better than I've imagined.*

Amen.

The Man of My Dreams

Essentials:

1. That he is a solid Christian whose foundation is built on the Word of God
2. That his heart's desire is to serve Christ with his whole being
3. That the order of the household is God, wife and kids, ministry
4. That he has a sense of humor
5. That he is a good communicator
6. That he is good with people
7. That he wants children and knows how to discipline them

Non-Essentials:

1. That he is taller than me (noticeably!)
2. That he is a preacher
3. That he is an athlete
4. That he can sing
5. That he is a pastor's son
6. That he has a good relationship with his mother
7. That he sometimes wears glasses
8. That he likes to travel

*   *   *

We sat side-by-side in the airport terminal waiting for our flight. Jennie and I were two of more than a dozen team members heading to Honduras for Spring Break my junior year of college. The rest of our group spread out around the waiting area near our gate. Some played cards, some talked in groups, but Jennie and I sat silently. We were both distracted by what we were watching.

At the check-in counter at our gate, a couple stood talking to the airport employee. Young and attractive, they held hands and smiled at each other. It seemed they were on their way to a honeymoon destination.

Jennie and I must have both arrived at this same assumption about these apparent newlyweds because we looked at each other simultaneously and both sighed as we said, "Someday . . ." Then we giggled at our simultaneous reactions.

Having female friends to dream with and talk to was a gift of the single-girl season. We'd spent many conversations in the dorm discussing our dreams of marriage. We just hoped we didn't have to wait much longer to be sitting beside our new husbands instead of each other.

Later on that same trip, as we helped to build and paint a small church for a poor community in Honduras, I once again stopped and watched. This time I observed the entire scene around me. Friends and a respected college professor worked hard in the heat and noise. I stood still and listened.

Hammers beat on boards. A broom scraped dust across a dirt floor. The laughter of children who had come to watch the white people work floated around me. Both Spanish and English mingled in my ears.

And a song came to mind. I did not break out singing it. I just stood and listened to it in my mind. The lyrics became a prayer. They spoke of loving the Lord and lifting my voice to worship Him. They spoke of the Lord taking joy in what He heard. I had always thought of those lyrics in light of the singing of the song itself and the sound of voices in chapel or church. But, this time, I listened to the sounds of work being done, labor and love at its finest. And I asked God to take joy in the sounds that He heard. The sounds of life. The sounds of hammering, and working, and talking, and laughing. Of love and serving. The sounds of God's people living in ways to honor Him.

And I committed again to live my life in a way that honored God. No matter what that meant.

I desperately wanted to meet "Mr. Right" and marry him, but for now, I stood in a tiny community surrounded by mountains in Honduras. I did not want to waste this season of singleness. I did not want to wish it away in hopes for "someday."

*   *   *

In a matter of weeks after college graduation, my life blurred into children's ministry, especially my Sunday mornings.

I oversaw the infants through fifth graders at Emmanuel Community Church, where my dad pastored, and where I'd attended since I was ten years old (other than a year when I interned at another church in Nappanee, Indiana). Now I'd been charged with leading the children, at least while they were at church, and I took my job seriously.

The church had grown quite a bit since the days of the gravel driveway and red carpeted rooms behind the sanctuary in 1989. Now the church was averaging 800 attendees each Sunday and its structure had also grown after the completion of two large building projects.

I enjoyed teaching the children, as well as overseeing and training the more than seventy weekly adult volunteers who made the ministry possible. The church was still growing and getting ready to expand to three

Sunday morning services.

Sitting in a staff meeting one day, leadership asked me if I'd like to start teaching a Sunday school class for "Twenty-somethings." The thought of an hour spent with people my own age (during which it was highly unlikely that anyone would ask me to take them to the potty) enticed me. However, my Sunday mornings were already packed full of responsibility. I mulled it over and finally said that if the staff could find someone to co-teach with me I'd be willing to give it a try.

Little did I know there was a man named Kraig Cabe who had moved to Fort Wayne less than two years before and who oversaw a ministry new to the area called the Fellowship of Christian Athletes. FCA is a worldwide ministry organization, but our area in Indiana lacked a director for years prior to Kraig taking the Northern Indiana position. Kraig had attended a local church plant after first moving to town, but, eventually, with some help from the Indiana Pacers, wound up at Emmanuel Community Church.

*   *   *

One evening, Kraig, a single, poor, twenty-six-year-old in full-time ministry, wanted to watch the NBA playoffs but couldn't afford cable in his apartment. So he went to Applebee's and sat in the bar and ordered a string of Sprites to get him through a game of the Knicks versus his team, the Indiana Pacers.

Kraig noticed that another man sitting beside him in the bar was cheering for the Knicks and drinking an awful lot of soda. The two struck up a conversation about basketball and life that eventually led the typical, "What do you do?" question.

Kraig said, "Well, I feel a little awkward telling you this while sitting in the bar, but I'm in full-time ministry with the Fellowship of Christian Athletes."

"Oh! That's no problem!" said Dave Riddle. "I'm a pastor!"

The two hit it off and by the end of the evening Dave invited Kraig to try the church where he served as a pastoral intern, Emmanuel Community.

The Lord was setting up the best "guy walks into a bar" punchline of my life.

*   *   *

Kraig began attending Emmanuel and eventually had lunch with the senior pastor—my dad. They discussed many things over chips and salsa at Carlos O' Kelly's, including the fact that the church was much larger than what Kraig was used to attending, and that he'd like to get "plugged in" to serving so he could connect with people.

There just happened to be this "Twenty-something" class in need of a co-teacher.

*   *   *

I was sitting outside on my parents' deck getting ready to enjoy the dinner my mom had made. This was one of the many perks of moving back in with my parents after college graduation. I didn't plan to live there forever, but for these first few months, at least, I could save some rent money and enjoy the comforts of my old bedroom.

My dad joined us at the table and after we prayed he said, "Well, I think I had lunch with my future son-in-law today."

Ugh.

Enough already. I knew my parents were excited for me to find a man (and officially leave the nest), and I had endured much teasing throughout the years.

But this one was different.

Dad went on to explain that he'd had lunch with Kraig Cabe who worked for the Fellowship of Christian Athletes and that something about Kraig had really struck him. Kraig just reminded him of me and that he couldn't help but think we'd really hit it off.

And apparently my dad was not the only one who felt this way.

During the next several months, countless people at ECC would say to me, "Have you met Kraig Cabe? He's the nicest guy. I really think you two would like each other."

Yes, thank you. I got the memo.

I wasn't holding my breath. But I did file these conversations in the back of my mind.

I wondered how this Kraig Cabe would stack up against my list.

*   *   *

I was told that I'd start teaching the "Twenty-somethings" class (which by now had been dubbed the "Young Adults") that fall with this Kraig fellow. However, we hadn't yet met each other.

I remember passing a guy in the hallway at church one Sunday morning that summer, who I knew must have been Kraig, but we didn't speak and he didn't notice me (which unfortunately became a theme between us for awhile).

That August, the Young Adult Class hosted a kick-off pool party at the home of a family from the church whose daughter was about my age.

The day of the party I was at a home where I had been staying as a house sitter. That morning I knelt alone in their living room in front of their couch and I prayed. I prayed that as I met Kraig Cabe later that day that God would direct our new Sunday school class and our relationship.

Whatever that relationship might be.

A few hours later, I was chatting with some of the others when Kraig walked up in his dress slacks and polo shirt, fresh from a meeting. I was finally meeting this man about whom I'd heard so much.

And I was standing there in my bathing suit.

life morsel: Enjoy today. Pray about tomorrow.

six

humble pie and wedding cake

how I came to eat them both

The pool party went off flawlessly, and by the end of the evening I was interested in this Kraig Cabe.

Interested, indeed.

I wanted to learn more about this man who, so far, had lived up to the hype surrounding him. Of course, I hadn't been able to glean much information about Kraig at a pool party, complete with snacks and a group game of Trivial Pursuit, but clearly this guy was dating potential.

At 6'1", he stood taller than me. I could check that one requirement off the list. He also had a great smile and an endearing sincerity about him. His best Trivial Pursuit category had been "Sports and Leisure," which was fine by me and seemed to indicate he was a "man's man," which I thought a plus.

We'd laughed about the same things and he'd sat beside me on the folding metal chairs in the basement and never mentioned a girlfriend, so he was seemingly unattached.

So far, so good.

Much later I found out that during Trivial Pursuit, when we'd been answering questions about the Boston Bruins, Kraig decided he liked my legs. But, since we weren't playing Truth or Dare I unfortunately didn't learn this tidbit of information for many, many months.

I sure wish I had learned it then. It would have been a great consolation prize.

For, even though Kraig was unattached that August day, and for the next six months of our growing friendship, I didn't win the "girlfriend" title.

And despite the fact that Kraig unknowingly continued to meet the criteria in both columns of my list, like the time he showed up at my office to chat and was wearing glasses (nice!), I never told him how I felt, and he never asked me out. Later I'd learn that Kraig thought I was too young, at the age of twenty-two, for his twenty-six years.

But each day I continued to pray for God's will in our lives, and I asked for God to please include a plan involving Kraig Cabe and Christy Miller in "couple status."

I prayed, hoped . . . and thought we were headed toward an answer to my prayers.

But Kraig saw me solely as a friend. With nice legs.

*   *   *

I enjoy being creative and making crafts, and decided that year to paint Christmas ornaments to give as gifts to friends and family. I bought plain round ornaments with a slight white frost to them and I added my own design to each. For each recipient, I wrote their name around the sphere and then I painted a strand of Christmas lights that wrapped around the letters. Though simple, they made cute gifts for my friends. I made one for Kraig, too. I had known him then for about five months, and considered him a friend.

Our Young Adult group was meeting at the church for a Christmas get-together. I had several small gift bags prepared and waiting in my office for the friends I'd see at the get-together. Each contained the handmade ornament with their name on it.

I knew Kraig would soon be coming in and so I grabbed his gift bag and met him in the lobby. I gave him the gift. He opened it and saw the ornament that I'd carefully painted. "Thanks," he said tentatively. Then he added, "Would you mind keeping this here in your office? I'm afraid if I put it in my car it might break from being in the cold."

"Sure," I said quickly and took it back. I placed it back in the gift bag, rallied my emotions enough to put a smile on my face and act like this direct return of a gift didn't bother me. But it stung. I didn't know quite what Kraig was thinking, but I felt as if he was rejecting my gift. I doubted he was truly concerned that the temperature would damage the ornament. I placed the gift bag on top of a filing cabinet in my office where it sat for several weeks before Kraig eventually did take it with him one day when he left the church building. Apparently, the weather had improved enough to provide a safe car ride home for the glass gift.

Many months later, perhaps after we were married, I asked Kraig what he had been thinking that evening and why he did not just accept the gift. He confessed that he thought I was flirting with him by making him a homemade ornament, that it seemed forward of me. He didn't realize that I had given them to other people as well, not just him.

I had feared he was thinking this. And it irked me. I couldn't believe that Kraig would choose to potentially hurt my feelings with this backhanded rejection rather than choosing kindness, regardless of what he thought my motive was.

I was also hurt because though I had been pretty smitten with Kraig from the day we met at the pool party, I never blatantly flirted with him. I was absolutely not forward with him or pushy. Instead, I chose to remain his friend, and to treat him with kindness and respect, just like I would treat any other friend. I wanted him to like me for who I was, not some "act" I could put on in front of him.

Am I still a little bitter about this? Perhaps.

But, we still have that little ornament, and fifteen Christmases later, I make sure to hang it on the tree, front and center, every year.

*   *   *

The late February morning when I sat in my office starkly contrasted the summer afternoon pool party where we'd met seven months earlier. I had been so patient. I was kind about the returning of the handmade ornament and though I really liked Kraig, I refrained from flirting or pushing him toward a romantic relationship. But, despite the waiting, my hopes remained high. I saw great potential for us. I figured Kraig was slower to notice, but that he would soon come around and realize he had feelings for me beyond our friendship.

This day, I learned I was wrong.

I heard my email "ding" and my heart began to pound when I saw Kraig's name listed as the sender. The email suggested plans for an upcoming date!

Then I realized the email wasn't meant for me. My excitement spiraled into confusion, realization, and devastation.

Oh, it was addressed to my email address, but intended for a different recipient: the girl whom Kraig was dating.

I didn't know Kraig *was* dating anyone, and the fact I'd learned via an email instead of through what I perceived to be a good friendship bothered me.

That I wasn't the girl he'd chosen nearly broke my heart.

I pushed reply and typed, "I think you might have meant this for someone else. Have a great day!"

And then I remembered I was at work and needed to move on with my own day. And my life.

I sat still in my desk chair and blinked rapidly trying to hold back the tears that stung my eyes.

I decided after awhile that I needed something to help with the pain, so I ran an errand—to Walmart to restock the preschool supply of goldfish crackers.

And while at the store I washed down my sorrows with a frozen Coke.

*   *   *

I didn't want to like her.

She was the girl dating the guy whom I had prayed would be mine. But I did like her.

I didn't know Kraig's girlfriend previously, but I came to know her in the almost nine months that they dated. Kraig brought his girlfriend to almost all of our Young Adult Class social events and so there she was, hanging out with the rest of us, dating the guy of my dreams right in front of me.

She was sweet, and kind, and Kraig treated her well.

All signs during those nine months pointed to their eventual marriage. It hurt me. Most people didn't realize how hard it was for me to be around the happy couple since I, myself, had never dated Kraig or even made my interest known.

My family knew, though. My parents and my brother and my brother's girlfriend all knew my feelings for Kraig. They said nothing to Kraig, but watched me during those months, recognizing my disappointment.

I began to change the way I prayed.

Instead of asking for Kraig to be mine, I asked that he'd move away, or at least away from my weekly routine of teaching alongside him and leading social events with our class. It was just too hard. My feelings for Kraig didn't change; it would be better if he simply left my life instead of marrying another girl in front of me.

I also decided that I needed to move on by dating other guys. Odd to "get over" a guy I had never actually dated, but I needed to do it. So, I allowed friends to set me up on blind dates. I actually went on several dates with a guy who lived in Indianapolis, about two hours away. He was a nice guy and we enjoyed ourselves on our dates. We spent time in Fort Wayne and Indianapolis, and I truly had fun. But then I broke up with him. I didn't see the potential for a long-term relationship, and why waste my time and gasoline?

Then I accepted a blind date with another guy. One lunch was enough to rule out that one. Sorry, but no thanks.

I wanted to move on. I was trying. It didn't help.

Then one weekend in early November, the FCA hosted a high school retreat weekend in southern Indiana. Kraig needed a female "huddle leader," someone to lead the girls' small group meetings during the retreat, and he asked me if I'd be interested. Kraig and I, along with three other guys and two other girls who were also volunteering, rode down together to the camp. Kraig's girlfriend stayed home.

The weekend went well, and I enjoyed working with the high school girls and seeing the ministry impact of FCA. I had attended other FCA events throughout the previous year and had always appreciated Kraig's leadership and heart for the ministry.

In fact, I laugh now to think about some of my first impressions of FCA. Shortly after meeting Kraig, I attended one of his annual fundraising banquets, and I'd taken my mom as a guest. We both sat at the round table during the meal and discussed how we thought Kraig did a great job and the event's purpose was wonderful, but aesthetically, it really needed a "woman's touch." Little did we know then that we would both become those women who decorated and helped with FCA banquets for years to come! What's that saying? "Be the change you want to see?" Well, we now are.

After a successful retreat, the group of us rode home together in a big blue van. We laughed and chatted and at one point the conversation turned to what each of us wanted in a future spouse (only one of us was already married at the time). Kraig was driving and I was sitting in the middle captain's chair behind the passenger seat as I listened to him state characteristics he was looking for in a wife.

Later, some of the other friends who were along for that ride told me that it appeared so obvious that we should be a couple it seemed almost funny. But that day, I simply sat there, silent, listening to Kraig, and to the screaming voice in my head, "Hello! Look over your right shoulder. Don't you see? The girl who meets all of those criteria is sitting *right behind you?!*"

*   *   *

It turns out the voice in Kraig's head muttered some similar thoughts to the voice in mine.

He couldn't help but realize that when he'd needed someone to help him in his ministry his first choice had been me. He'd been impressed with how I'd handled the Young Adult class and now FCA events, and he was starting to see me as more than just a Sunday school class co-teacher. Feelings for me sprouted, a little confusing given the fact that he had a serious girlfriend.

Soon after returning from the FCA high school retreat, Kraig and his girlfriend had a pivotal conversation. She asked him a barbed question,

"If you weren't dating me, would you be dating Christy Miller?" She said she could see us together. Kraig's answer wasn't exactly the romantic response she was hoping to hear. "Well, there'd be no red flags," he said, and with that their relationship began to come apart. I had no idea.

The following Saturday evening, our Young Adult class held a game night and my parents offered to host it. We all sat on the family room floor playing *Catch Phrase!*. I was on Kraig's right and his girlfriend sat on his left. I was still certain that Kraig would propose to her any day, and so I focused on playing the game and enjoying our group of friends. I laughed a lot and enjoyed the evening. Unbeknownst to me, Kraig and his girlfriend were not feeling so carefree. The evening ended late and everyone headed his or her own way.

Kraig and his girlfriend headed back to his apartment and broke up.

I headed to bed that night happy I'd gotten to play *Catch Phrase!*. I like that game.

Sunday morning, November 11, I stood in the doorway of my fifth grade classroom where I taught Jr. Discipleship the hour before our Young Adult class met. Kraig came to the door before my class began and asked if he could talk to me for a minute. He looked tired.

I let my fifth graders talk among themselves for a moment while I prepared to listen to whatever Kraig wanted to tell me. Maybe he had an idea for our lesson later that morning.

"Christy, you're going to have to help me when I teach this morning. I'm really tired and I didn't get to prepare as I hoped."

Sure. I'd be happy to.

"I was up late because my girlfriend and I broke up last night."

On the outside, I said something about helping however I could and I was calmly shaking my head, putting on an empathetic expression to show Kraig I was sorry.

On the inside, I was turning cartwheels and beaming.

*   *   *

That very afternoon after church our Young Adult class played bingo at a nursing home. Bingo or not, I was winning that day.

As we left the nursing home, Kraig asked me if I would come up to his office that evening to help him set up for a board meeting he had the following morning.

"I want to tell you what we talked about last night when we broke up. I think you'll be interested."

That may have been an understatement.

I told him I'd meet him in an hour at his office.

Later that day, I walked into his office building and met him in a classroom where he was to hold the board meeting. The "set up" for the meeting involved pushing two tables together and laying some pens on them. I was pretty sure Kraig could have handled that on his own.

"You may want to sit," Kraig said, pointing to one of the chairs at the corner of the table. I did and Kraig sat right around the corner facing me. A board meeting of two commenced.

"I wanted to tell you what we talked about last night when we broke up," he continued. "We actually talked about you."

"Okay . . . " I said slowly, not sure where this was going.

Kraig explained the conversations they'd been having about the idea of him dating me, and how he'd had no reservations about the thought, other than he had a girlfriend. Though his girlfriend was heartbroken, they ended the relationship because Kraig decided he didn't see their relationship progressing any further.

My throat tightened. My pulse quickened.

All in favor say AYE!

Kraig continued, "So, I was wondering if you'd ever considered the idea of us dating."

Those opposed?

I smiled and said, "Yes, I've definitely considered us dating. I'd like that."

And then I said something I still regret to this day. In fact, when I think about it I feel the need to slap my own forehead. Repeatedly.

"In fact," I continued, "my dad even said when he first met you that he thought you may someday be his son-in-law."

As soon as the words left my mouth I knew I'd said too much. The color drained from Kraig's face. I thought with that one statement I'd blown my chance with this guy forever.

But to his credit, he rallied, and slowly recovered.

After a few moments of stunned silence Kraig said, "Well, I'm going home for Thanksgiving next week and I want a couple of weeks to tell my family about breaking up with my girlfriend and everything. I'll call you in a few weeks and we'll go out. Okay?"

"Okay," I said. "I'll look forward to it."

We smiled at each other and talked some more before I drove home with my head in the clouds.

Meeting adjourned.

*   *   *

True to his word, Kraig called me about two weeks later and asked me out on our first date. Though unsure about the transition from being co-teachers, and friends, to girlfriend and boyfriend, the shift happened easily and as natural as could be.

That first night, November 29, 2001, we enjoyed dinner at a local Italian restaurant, Biaggi's, and a movie. The next night we went Christmas caroling with our Young Adult class as a couple. The rumors began to fly. Actually, they were true.

Kraig and Christy were a couple. My prayers had been answered.

*   *   *

My Grandma Miller, who had earlier suggested I cross some desired qualities off of my "future husband wish list," agreed that the little she knew of Kraig, indeed, appeared to meet the high standards I had set. While she and I were shopping one day and standing in a clothing store near the neatly folded shirts and sweaters, I told her that Kraig and I were a couple. She held church right then and there as she raised her hands and sang "Hallelujah!"

Can I get an amen?

About seven months into our relationship, which was going wonderfully, Kraig accompanied my extended family on a summer vacation where fourteen of us stayed together in a lake house in Virginia. Kraig shared a room with my brother, Nate, and my cousin, Justin. The guys played Stratego, got Frisbees stuck on the roof, and competed in water sports behind the speedboat. I loved watching them interact. Kraig was enjoying my family as well and told me months later that he decided on that trip that he could not only spend the rest of his life with me, but also would genuinely like the family he'd gain.

Grandma Miller, who was also along for the Virginia vacation, chimed in with her two cents about Kraig again as she and I sat on a porch swing and watched the guys throw a Frisbee in the yard. "Christy, some guys have those skinny little chicken legs, but not Kraig. He has really nice legs." I looked over at her with raised eyebrows. After a pause, I burst out laughing and promptly shared this interesting conversation with the rest of the family. Kraig considered wearing long pants the remainder of the trip.

A couple of months later, I began hoping that we'd marry, but we hadn't discussed timing or rings or anything.

On the Thursday before Labor Day weekend, 2002, Kraig took the day off and went golfing with my dad. I thought it a little strange that he'd take a day off and not spend it with me, but had I known his intent, I would have been thrilled. Kraig was asking my dad for permission to marry me.

Kraig was a nervous wreck during the first five holes at Cherry Hill Golf Course. He was trying to think of a way to bring up the topic. But finally, while they sat in the cart before the sixth hole, which happens to be an island green surrounded by water, Kraig said, "Well, there was a reason I asked you to golf today."

He asked my dad if he could marry his only daughter. My dad said yes. He was thrilled for us! And then Dad proceeded to hit his tee-shot into the water.

*   *   *

Friday, August 30, Kraig and I planned a day-long date at Lake Webster where his parents and aunt and uncle shared a speedboat they docked there. We planned to go up, just the two of us, and take the boat out on the lake for an afternoon of reading and picnicking.

Kraig remembers watching me make peanut butter and jelly sandwiches that morning and my excitement about the Ding Dongs I was packing. I was really looking forward to the day (and the Ding Dongs!). He smiled inside, thinking I had no idea just how special this day would be.

We took the boat out onto the middle of the lake and read our books and chatted on that beautiful late summer day.

Kraig kept asking me if I was ready to eat lunch. At 10:30 in the morning.

Later he told me that he figured we'd better eat before he proposed or else I'd be too excited to eat afterward. You have to give the guy credit for thinking that far in advance. I really like Ding Dongs.

So, after our mid-morning "lunch" on the boat, Kraig told me, "I have a game I want you to play." He knew I liked games.

I laid on my stomach, propped up on my elbows on the back of the boat and looked at the piece of paper Kraig had given me. He also gave me a pen and told me to fill in the blanks.

I was up to the challenge.

There were six questions complete with blanks:

Razzle is to Dazzle as _____ is to Cross.

Easy. *Criss.*

Don't go, but _____ here with me.

Got it. *Stay*

What is the largest sea mammal?

Well, I'm not an expert, but I'm pretty sure it's a *Whale.*

... but the poor man had nothing except one little _____ *lamb he had bought. 2 Samuel 12:3*

Again, I'm pretty sure the word he left out is *Ewe*

A female horse?

I think it's a *Mare*

And finally, Who is Robert's girlfriend on the show, *Everybody Loves Raymond?*

Oh, I love that show! It's *Amy*

Kraig told me that I had gotten all of the answers correct.

Great! I thought. So what?

"Now play *Mad Gab* with your answers," Kraig said.

We'd played *Mad Gab* before and I usually figured out what phrase or expression the group of words being said aloud together was supposed to sound like.

So I took the six words I had just written and said them together out loud.

"CRISS STAY WHALE EWE MARE AMY"

As soon as I said it, I heard it.

I had just said, "Christy, will you marry me?"

My jaw dropped and I turned my head to the left to see the man I loved, the man I'd first met while wearing my bathing suit at a pool party, wearing his swim trunks and down on one knee in the middle of a speedboat. He held an open velvet box. A beautiful diamond ring sparkled in the bright sunlight.

I sat up with wide-eyes and mouth open as Kraig said, "Christy Miller, will you marry me?"

"No way! No way!" I kept repeating, shocked at the wonderful surprise he'd pulled off. After I wrapped my head around the moment, I quickly adjusted my answer.

"Yes! I'll marry you!"

Kraig hugged me and said the words we hadn't in the nine months of dating. Words we both had wanted to reserve for the one person we knew we'd spend the rest of our lives with.

"I love you, Christy Miller. You don't know how much I love you."

The feeling was absolutely mutual.

life morsel: Love is a gift. Give and receive it freely.

The day we got engaged! Kraig had this vase of roses delivered to the table during our celebratory dinner. The card read, "I love you!"

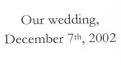

Our wedding, December 7th, 2002

seven

dark chocolate

how life mimicked its bittersweet combination

Our December evening wedding sparkled with pure white lights. The garland that lined the sanctuary walls flickered with soft twinkles. A large tree graced the front of the room near the stage and a shining star adorned its top. A few smaller fake trees, on which we'd wrapped white lights, sat on the platform behind the wedding party. My mom lit a floral-scented candle in the foyer, the beautiful fragrance swirled in our noses as the ambience of love pulsated in our hearts. Outside, the skies remained clear all afternoon until snow fluttered down like confetti at nightfall.

I will never forget the look on Kraig's face as I walked down the aisle toward him. His smile stretched across his face; his eyes glowed. It may have taken him longer than it took me to realize that we were meant for each other, but no doubt clouded either of our minds anymore.

My off-the-shoulder wedding dress made me feel like a princess. I looked around and smiled at my girlfriends who agreed to stand up as my attendants in eggplant-colored dresses. The guys stood straight and sharp in their black tuxes. The large congregation of about 450 in attendance brought energy and excitement as they sang along with the songs we had chosen for the ceremony, and as they laughed and cried, as if on cue, during several moments of the vows and message, I knew I could not have scripted a dream any better.

We spent our honeymoon in Hawaii where a friend offered us the use of his condominium as his wedding gift to us. Truly, we were blessed beyond measure.

We also began life together as homeowners. Before the wedding, while I lived with my parents in Roanoke, Kraig lived in a small apartment in Fort Wayne. This bachelor pad offered little aesthetic value, other than the good-looking man who lived there. The refrigerator usually held a large jar of strawberry jelly, some milk, and a case of Pepsi. The freezer contained a "delicacy" with which I was unfamiliar, frozen Chips Ahoy cookies. Kraig liked to eat them when they were in a state hard enough to chip a tooth. In the cupboard resided the peanut butter and the bread. But we remember the counter in Kraig's apartment for one thing. An orange sprinkle. And I wasn't even there to see it.

Before Kraig and I dated, he had hosted his parents, brother and sister-in-law, and their two young boys for an evening. The family bought doughnuts for a treat, and being October, Kraig's little nephew, Kordell, ordered a doughnut topped with festive orange sprinkles. He ate it by the counter in Uncle Kraig's apartment.

A couple of months later, the family once again visited Kraig's apartment for an evening. Kordell climbed up to the counter and said, "Look, Uncle Kraig! It's my sprinkle!" The orange sprinkle still lay where Kordell had dropped it months before.

When I heard this story, I understood that Kraig didn't expect a china-and-linen lifestyle. Plus it took the pressure off my housekeeping skills! Though I was no Betty Crocker or Martha Stewart, I could at least wipe off a counter from time to time. And, possibly learn to cook as well.

With that in mind, we decided to use the money we had both been saving on a house down payment. We found a cute little ranch in Fort Wayne and made an offer.

The evening we closed on the house, after the keys were in our pockets and the previous owner's possessions gone, we walked through with smiles on our faces. Our home. The Cabe home. I liked the sound of that.

Kraig and I knelt in the empty kitchen that evening and held hands. We prayed together that our home would be full of two things: joy and peace. We also prayed that everyone who would fill its rooms, including future children, would know they were both welcome and loved.

Our happily ever after had begun.

*   *   *

I owned a home, had a husband, received monthly utility bills, and grew excited about organizing my closet space. I was a certified grown-up.

As a rookie adult, I began to see certain things from a new perspective. For example, planning holiday gatherings no longer meant only the fun of seeing loved ones, but the responsibility of what food to bring, and the concern about both sides of the family receiving "equal time."

Homeownership brought new challenges and perspectives as well, beyond the need to ensure the mortgage payment. One time, an awful smell assaulted Kraig and I from our hallway bathroom. Tree roots had clogged our sewer line, the one that ran under our front yard to the street's sewer system, and the pipe had collapsed. Sewage could no longer travel its usual route so it found an alternative path into our home through small openings in our bathtub drain and toilet seal. Obviously, this caused an awful stench and it needed to be handled immediately. But, spending a bundle on the installation of a new drainage pipe under our destroyed front lawn didn't factor into my newlywed dreams. Since I also didn't wish to convert to using an outhouse, the forced improvement project became "just part of being an adult."

These "you're an adult, now" changes popped up in many aspects. For the most part, I took them in stride and enjoyed the season of young adulthood very much. I had looked forward to it!

Some of these natural changes in perspective were tangible (that's a nice word for the sewage issue), but I also gained some perspective changes that were mostly emotional and intellectual. New thought patterns ran through my mind and created alternative paths where ideas and feelings seeped in.

One of these shifts had begun to sprout my sophomore year of college. A shift in my feelings about my mom's death and my dad's remarriage.

I was still 100-percent in love with my second mom, Karin, and I didn't wish for any change or distancing in our relationship. In fact, I had only come to love her more deeply and appreciated her very much. However, I had experienced the loss of my mom and the remarriage of my dad through a child's eyes. Now, I was growing adult eyes and this changed my focus.

As a child, a sixth grader, I wanted my dad to remarry quickly because I basically thought we needed help. My brother and I needed a mom, and Dad needed a wife. I didn't want to eat cereal for supper until I was eighteen, and more so, I wanted a mom to love me, and for me to have another mom to love.

As a child, I didn't understand the social norms about remarriage after the death of a spouse. That many people saw Dad's remarriage, less than seven months after my mom's death, as really fast.

Now as a fledgling adult, I sat in my dorm room and counted on my fingers the months between my mom's death, and the wedding of my dad and Karin. I was shocked. Wow! I thought. *What was Dad thinking? How could he have done that?* I spent several weeks of my sophomore year grieving my mom's death again, this time as a young adult. I missed her in a fresh way. I wanted to know her and spend time with her. While difficult, I believe it was important for me to face this head-on and to walk through it, not around.

I talked through this grief with my parents. They mostly listened, but they also answered the questions I asked about their own perspective and memories of dating and that general time in our lives. They had known their relationship and marriage was considered fast as it was happening. This was not news to them. But they patiently discussed it again these years later, and that helped me to process my own thoughts and feelings. Now, the idea of losing a spouse took on new meaning since I was married myself.

As a newlywed who was head over heels in love with her new husband, I couldn't imagine how hard my mom's death must have been on my dad. My heart broke for him anew.

I also began to fear that something would happen to Kraig. My relationship with ambulance sirens still haunted me, and any time Kraig was not home and I'd hear a siren, I'd fear the worst. I'm embarrassed to admit that, on many occasions, I'd call him just to hear him say "Hello," and to know he was all right. When he began to understand my "siren issue," he took the initiative to call me first if he was near our home and heard a siren. "I thought you might be able to hear that siren right now and I just wanted you to know that I'm okay," he'd say. I loved him even more for his empathy.

Perspective changes everything. And as an adult I gained some new views of the world. How I saw my very own master bedroom closet. The bills Kraig and I now paid each month. The dirt piled high in our front yard by crews fixing our sewer line. (A neighbor friend planted a sign in the dirt,

"Mount Cabe—highest point in the neighborhood." Sometimes new perspectives need a little signage for clarification. And a little humor can help adjust our attitudes.)

Fresh adult eyes simply focused differently than my childhood eyes had. My understanding of loss, grief, and love evolved.

With this grew an overwhelming sense of gratitude for what had been, along with great anticipation for what was to come.

*　　*　　*

Though five negative pregnancy tests lined my trash cans, my instincts and body argued otherwise. We had been married just over a year.

After two weeks of waiting, a new family doctor finally fit me in for an appointment. The nurse administered yet another pregnancy test and asked me to wait in the little room for the doctor. But before the doctor had a chance to come in, the nurse stuck her head in the door. "It's positive!" she said with a smile.

I slowly let her words sink in to my mind and my heart. I was pregnant!

After meeting with the doctor and finding out I was about six weeks along, I drove, on a snowy January highway, to Kraig's office. We shut his office door for privacy, and I told him the news. We were overjoyed!

The next morning I began bleeding. I saw the doctor again. This time she was somber. "I'm sorry, but I think you are miscarrying," she said. "There is really nothing we can do but wait."

And wait I did. For an entire week I bled, yet I still experienced nausea. An ultrasound scheduled for my seventh week of pregnancy would let us see a heartbeat, if there was one. The doctor was doubtful. Kraig and

I earnestly prayed God would spare this child. We also prayed for God's will to prevail most all.

As I lay on the table and watched the little screen, a tiny heartbeat fluttered away. Kraig and I almost burst with excitement. The baby had survived. It was growing and thriving.

I carried this child to forty-one weeks gestation and gave birth to a 9 lb., 10 oz. baby boy we named Karson Andrew.

After the initial chaos of the delivery room settled down and the nurses left the room, I lay in the bed holding my swaddled son. Kraig stood on our right with his Bible open to Psalm 139. He read verses 13-16 aloud to his brand new boy:

> "For you created my inmost being; you knit me together in my mother's womb. I praise you because I am fearfully and wonderfully made; your works are wonderful, I know that full well. My frame was not hidden from you when I was made in the secret place, when I was woven together in the depths of the earth. Your eyes saw my unformed body; all the days ordained for me were written in your book before one of them came to be."

We did not know what God had in store for Karson, but we trusted that God had already ordained his days, and we were thrilled to be along for the ride as his parents.

* * *

Words could never adequately describe the joy I receive from being a mom. Motherhood changed my life in many ways, including now staying home full-time instead of working, more interrupted sleep . . . and meals . . .

and trips to the bathroom for that matter. But I was smitten with motherhood, and even more so with Karson.

Karson delighted me. Though he struggled with digestive issues and was fussier than many babies in his early months, I lived in a sleepy bliss. And even though I struggled greatly with giving up nursing him when the doctor advised us to try a special formula for his issues, it did make a positive difference. Karson's tummy agreed, and he was soon a consistently happy baby. He smiled easily, loved to laugh, and met all milestones perfectly. He took his first steps at home while holding a small basketball and toddling toward a tiny hoop where he literally made his first ever layup. A proud moment for his Hoosier parents.

Kraig and I loved parenthood so much that we decided we wanted to have another baby sooner rather than later. And shortly after Karson turned one, I was pregnant again. But once again I started to bleed. This time the pain involved and the ensuing ultrasound indicated no signs of life. We lost that child to miscarriage and my heart hurt.

Two months later I was pregnant again. This time I guarded my heart even more and it turned out I was right to do so. We lost that child to miscarriage as well.

Miscarriage is a somewhat "invisible" grief as there is often no face and no name associated with the loss. Even if the parents do name their child, their friends and family feel very little connection to the child and cannot truly understand the depth of the loss. The grief of miscarriage feels lonely. It is the death of a dream. The death of what could have been.

We had a child. We lived in such happiness, but sadness joined our family of three as well, and it wasn't the addition we'd desired. Much like when I bite into a piece of dark chocolate, I experienced bitterness mingled with the sweet. Delightful moments sweetened our home. Times of mourning darkened it.

Kraig and I dealt with the losses in our own ways. He was sad, yet more matter-of-fact. I was emotional. I had been the only one to hold those children when I held them in my womb. They left a ragged void, sharp-edged and real.

When I was in high school, I took four years of Spanish. My dad knew almost no Spanish, but one evening at dinner, Dad mentioned a phrase from a radio advertisement for Spanish lessons.

"Do you know if you spell socks slowly you're saying a phrase in Spanish?" he said proudly. "S-O-C-K-S. It means, 'It is what it is.'"

I thought, one, this was cheating when it came to speaking Spanish. Not impressed. Two, I didn't know this phrase in English. "It is what it is." What was that supposed to mean?

Years later, when dealing with the grief of miscarriage, I began to understand. I had lost two children, two dreams, two "what could have beens." I could do nothing about it, except bear a lonely and invisible grief. I wanted a shortcut through this. I wanted an explanation for what had happened. I wanted to be done with the disappointment. But I learned that grief must be acknowledged. It can't be stuffed in the closet in hopes that it will never come back to haunt you. No, it is better to look it in the face and call it by its many names. It is loss. It is difficult. It is unfair. It is unbiased. It is sad. It is unpredictable.

It is what it is.

*   *   *

As a teenager, I had a problem with the Lord's Prayer. I supported it as a whole, but I just couldn't bring myself to say one line, "Thy kingdom come."

'Our Father which art in heaven,

Hallowed be thy name,

Thy kingdom come,

Thy will be done in earth,

as it is in heaven.

Give us this day our daily bread.

And forgive us our debts,

as we forgive our debtors.

And lead us not into temptation,

but deliver us from evil.

Matthew 6:9-13 (KJV)

Words matter to me. If I am going to recite a statement of belief, like the "Pledge of Allegiance," for example, I make sure I first agree with its content. When praying the Lord's Prayer, making a statement to Almighty God, you had better believe I am even more intent on the content. Therein lies the problem.

I was taught that praying "Thy kingdom come" basically was asking God to return and take me to heaven and end life as I knew it. I was good with all of that, except I didn't want it to happen . . . yet. I was a self-focused teenage girl with dreams. I wanted to get married and have kids first. Was that too much to ask? And so, out of a somewhat selfish, but mostly sincere heart, I would deliberately not speak those three words aloud whenever I prayed the Lord's Prayer. It was not often that I found myself in this situation, but sometimes our family would hold hands and say the Lord's Prayer aloud before dinner, maybe once or twice a month, instead of one of us praying our own prayer aloud. Due to the infrequency, I was able to avoid saying those three words fairly easily.

But as I aged it became more difficult. Both my circumstances and my heart began to change.

Now I was twenty-eight years old and my prayer prerequisites had been met. I was married and had become a mom. My dream was now my reality. Other than dealing with the miscarriages, the first several years of our marriage and journey into parenthood felt nearly perfect. Extreme happiness and contentment enveloped me.

So I began to say those three words aloud. "Thy kingdom come."

I gave God the green light to do what He needed to do when it came to His Kingdom. I figured I was ready for Heaven now and the end of life as I knew it.

But never did I imagine how my life would indeed soon change forever.

life morsel: Grief is what grief is. Acknowledging pain helps bring healing.

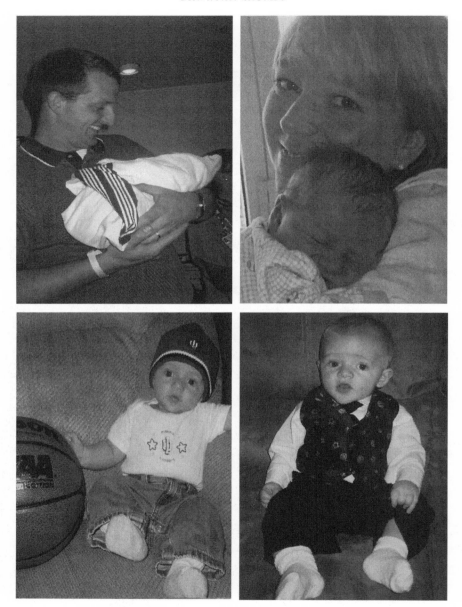

Top Left: Kraig holding his son for the first time

Top Right: I loved being a Mommy already!

Bottom Left: We live in Indiana, so a basketball picture is a must!

Bottom Right: Karson on the day of his baby dedication at church

Top Left: Karson on his first birthday

Top Right: Karson around two years old, before his diagnosis

Bottom: Three happy Cabes on Karson's second birthday

eight

an asparagus and chemotherapy

how they both impacted our life

He walked through the kitchen with an odd limp. Karson, just over two years old, played happily as usual, but occasionally complained, that February Saturday, that his legs hurt. We tried to think back to a fall or an injury, but drew a blank.

The next morning at church, Karson asked me to carry him to his classroom as we walked through the large foyer. I picked him up and made a mental note to talk to a nurse friend. When I did, Rebecca said that their policy at the pediatrician's office stated that a limp without a known injury should be checked out. She recommended a pediatric orthopedist, and I scheduled an appointment for the very next morning, a Monday. But first, that Sunday night we attended a Super Bowl party in my parents' basement where our team, the Indianapolis Colts, won the championship! Karson leaped off the couch, mostly unaware of the victory, but simply enjoying the party and adult attention, and moaned a little about his legs when he landed. Good thing this would be checked soon.

The orthopedist believed Karson had a hairline fracture in his leg. "We see this often with little boys. They play hard and injure themselves, and it causes a small fracture that will heal on its own. We don't even need to locate it at this point and we will not cast it or treat it. The only reason we would follow up is if Karson spikes a fever. A fever could indicate an infection in a joint. Call us if that happens."

I understood all of this. It made sense. We continued our week as planned.

On Wednesday, my mom and I took Karson to the mall. Karson did not feel up to walking, so we pushed him in the stroller and enjoyed the day with his otherwise cheerful self. While shopping, I wanted to look for some scrapbook supplies and found a small recording device that could be attached to a page and could hold a few seconds worth of sound bites. That evening I recorded Karson saying his name, age, and the phrase, "I love you." His sweet little voice played through the small speaker each time I pushed the button on the device. I also received in the mail that afternoon some photos I had sent away to be printed. I remember thinking what fun it would be to scrapbook these memories and how life seemed to be working out in a special way.

The next day, Thursday, Karson woke up with a low-grade fever and a runny nose. I was convinced we were dealing with a cold, not a joint infection that warranted a phone call to the doctor's office. But, when he still had a fever after his afternoon nap, I decided that I should call after all. The doctor asked that we go to our local hospital for a bone scan that evening. At this point he wanted to locate the fracture and rule out any infection. I gave Karson some children's ibuprofen and we drove to the hospital when Kraig arrived home from work.

The medicine perked Karson right back up to his normal, happy personality. I called the doctor's office once again and told them that I thought maybe we were wasting our time. The fever had gone down, and Karson was acting just fine. The nurse on the phone hesitated and said, "You're there. Why don't we just do this?"

A tech came into the room and drew Karson's blood. She took it from his arm and he handled it pretty well. Then it was time for the scan.

The technician operating the bone scan used a tape very similar to Duct tape to secure our two-year-old to the table. Karson had to lie still for forty minutes, but he handled it like a champ. The images we saw on the screen looked fine to us and we went home that evening believing we had a child with a cold and an achy leg. We crawled into bed that night and put this behind us.

The next morning, February 9, 2007, I took Karson for a follow-up appointment at the orthopedist's office to learn the official results of the scan. Because we anticipated it to be an "unimportant" appointment, Kraig went on to work.

I was wearing blue jeans, a white Adidas long-sleeved shirt with pink stripes down the arms, and tennis shoes with blue accents. The scenery of the day is burned into my mind.

After being weighed, Karson stood with the doctor and me in the hallway while the doctor put the scans up on the wall onto a lightbox. As we had suspected, no fracture could be found.

I began to believe that we must be dealing with something minor, maybe a possible infection that would require antibiotics. The doctor asked us to go into a small room and sit. He sat across from me and handed me two papers with the results of Karson's blood work on them. He pointed to some numbers and said, "Yes, see these things are off."

Huh? I had never read blood work before and did not know what I was looking at.

"If you'll excuse me, I am going to step out and call a colleague," the doctor said as he left the room. Still not overly concerned, I understood this man was an orthopedic doctor and not someone who regularly deals with blood counts. I figured he wanted to confirm something with a doctor who read these types of counts more routinely. I was right about that part.

While we waited, I entertained Karson by pulling a small blue spiral notebook out of my purse. I grabbed a pen and started drawing characters from the *Veggie Tales* movies and one of Karson's favorite characters of all time, Thomas the Tank Engine. I had just learned how to draw Thomas' face and was enjoying this practice. So was Karson.

The doctor returned and pulled a stool directly across from my chair. He sat.

"We think Karson has leukemia."

My world stopped. I sank in my own thoughts. Drowning in my confusion and concern. I tried to process what I'd been told, but I did not know how.

Finally, I said, "That's serious, right?"

"Thirty years ago it would have been a death sentence," the doctor went on as I tried to breathe. "But they have made a lot of medical advances. They can treat this now, but it's going to be a long, long road for you guys."

I still didn't understand. Leukemia. That was cancer, right?

"You need to call your husband. You both need to meet at home and pack your suitcases for at least a week. You have an appointment at Riley Hospital for Children in Indianapolis this afternoon at 2:00. Plan to stay for a while." A nurse had come into the room at some point and was now rubbing my back. It is never a good sign when a nurse goes out of her way to rub your back.

The doctor asked me to call Kraig. I stood and dialed his number on the corded phone that sat on the small counter nearby. Kraig answered. When I heard his voice, I crumbled. "The doctor needs to tell you something," I whimpered, unable to say the words myself. I handed the phone to the doctor who matter-of-factly explained things to Kraig. He handed the phone back to me, and Kraig and I spoke for a moment about meeting at home. It was all we could say.

I buckled Karson into his car seat in our minivan and then climbed in behind the wheel with sluggish movements. Kraig and I had just purchased the vehicle seven days earlier. Frustration soon joined my agony when I realized my gas tank was on empty. I pulled over at the nearest station and robotically began to fill up. I grabbed my cell phone and dialed my dad's number. My parents were out of town at a conference in Michigan. I didn't even think about that fact at that moment. Dad answered. I wept. Through sobs I broke the news to him. As I finished filling my tank, I kept talking and crying, and instinctively grabbed the printed receipt that was hanging from the pump. At the bottom of the receipt was the chipper sentence, "Have a nice day!"

I drove down the road through blurred vision. Dad told me repeatedly to be careful and then he said, "Christy, God has a plan in this. We have to trust Him." Then we made plans to meet that night at the hospital in Indianapolis.

After hanging up with my earthly father, I took a breath and cried out to my Heavenly Father—an anguished outcry that brought me hope. God was there. He heard my cries. He knew all about it already. And most of all, He loved me. That connection saved me in that moment.

Kraig and I met at home, and we hugged and cried for a long time. We aimlessly packed our bags and loaded back into our minivan. The two-hour drive to Riley Hospital was full of questions, tears, and phone calls. Kraig's parents were also heartbroken and on their way to meet us at Riley. While we drove along, we were also using our new van's DVD player and allowing an oblivious Karson to watch a *Veggie Tales* movie portraying the life of George Mueller. From the van speakers we heard an animated asparagus speak of trusting God to provide his needs every single day, and how every single day, God did. He tells the pea, "And this same God who takes care of me can supply all your needs from His glorious riches which have been given to us in Christ Jesus." Never had a conversation between two garden greens carried such impact in my life.

Before arriving at Riley Hospital for Children I knew two things about the place: it was in Indianapolis, and its logo featured a red wagon. Now I stood in its entrance and my son lay in a red wagon that I dragged down the hallway. The weight of the wagon was almost more than I could bear.

And so was the weight on my heart.

*　　*　　*

Numbness spread through my legs, a weakness that must have been obvious to those around me because a nurse pushed a stool behind my failing limbs and helped me to sit. I hadn't known how much I needed the support.

Karson was lying on the hospital bed, along with Lyle the Lamb, his stuffed companion. Kraig stood on the opposite side of the bed, rubbing Karson's little back. Our heads reeled. Wasn't it just this morning we had a normal life? Doctors were telling us that our toddler had cancer.

Denial joined shock. Kraig had been calling some of his colleagues from FCA and sharing the news. I kept telling him to stop because we might not be dealing with cancer here. Maybe it was just a cold. We shouldn't be sharing this news with non-family members until we knew for sure. But, my "Mommy heart" was the only one not accepting the leukemia diagnosis. Kraig's boss, who lived in Champaign, Illinois, drove several hours and sat in the waiting room that very evening and prayed. And though I never personally saw him that night, I will never forget his presence there.

Kraig's parents and my parents also arrived that afternoon and evening. I hugged my mother-in-law in the small procedure room and wept with her. The nurses were prepping Karson for a bone marrow biopsy.

Within my denial, I reasoned that if these trained medical professionals thought there was enough evidence of cancer from a small bit of blood work, then I must allow them to proceed with further testing of Karson's bone marrow. Maybe they could rule out cancer altogether. The doctors explained that leukemia starts in the marrow and they must take a look to find out what type of leukemia they were fighting. They also explained that marrow full of cancer cells would cause bone pain and be consistent with the leg pain and limping we had seen the last several days.

And so, in literally half a day, our normal routine had been hurled out and replaced with this dreaded procedure room in a hospital two hours from our house. I can smell the moment now.

Kraig used his forearms and physically pinned Karson down on that hospital bed as doctors used a large needle and tools to extract bone marrow from our little boy's hip. Karson was awake and acutely aware of the intense pain. As he lay there on his stomach, his face was turned toward his daddy who held him still and talked to him. Karson screamed and cried for the pain to stop.

He looked at Kraig with questioning eyes as if saying, "Why, Daddy?"

Crying.

"Why are you letting them hurt me?"

Crying.

"Please, Daddy, make it stop!"

How Kraig wanted to!

Kraig and I would have crawled onto that bed and taken that pain in a heartbeat rather than watch our son endure it. But we couldn't. The doctors had to proceed. We had to allow them to extract bone marrow so that they could determine what course of treatment would be most effective. But we couldn't explain all of that to a two-year-old. He wouldn't have understood.

And so as Karson screamed and pleaded with his daddy, all that Kraig could say in response was, "I love you, Karson."

Tears.

"I love you, buddy."

Tears.

"Oh, Karson! Daddy loves you so much!"

To this day, Kraig says that half hour was one of the most difficult times of his life. It was one of mine as well. Yet, as we have looked back on it, we are profoundly comforted by what it portrayed: the love between a father and his child.

How many times has my Heavenly Father held me down through pain, trial, sin and ugliness? I have not understood why, and probably wouldn't even if He told me. But when His face is turned toward me, much like when my own daddy's face was turned toward mine on our camping trip many years ago, I can look into His eyes and hear His words.

Daddy loves you.

I don't know why God allows pain in my life, or anyone else's. I simply do not know.

But I know my Father loves me. And that has been enough.

*   *   *

I sat on the edge of the bathtub and took the can of Sprite the nurse offered. Dr. Fallon had just delivered the news. I had been alone in Karson's room while the rest of the family was down in the Cancer Center playroom.

"We have gotten the bone marrow biopsy results. It is Acute Lymphoblastic Leukemia or A.L.L. This is actually good news. If you are going to have leukemia, this is the best type to have. I have treated this type of cancer hundreds of times, and I know exactly what to do."

My knees weakened, as if they would not hold my weight as I stood and listened. Dr. Fallon directed me to Karson's patient bathroom and helped me sit by the tub. He then asked a nurse to get me a drink.

My body gave out because my heart had finally caught up to the news. When Dr. Fallon stated the type of leukemia, my denial came to a crushing end. A type could not have been determined if it was not, in fact, leukemia. The diagnosis was true. As I finally accepted this fact, my body showed its displeasure at the sudden heaviness it was asked to bear.

After a few minutes and some tiny sips of Sprite, I walked down to the playroom and asked the family to listen to the news. Dr. Fallon, and the extremely patient nurses and physician assistants, took hours, during the course of our five-day stay, to explain to all of us what this diagnosis meant for Karson and our family.

When I stepped off the elevator onto the fifth floor that Friday night when our world was rocked, I disliked the place. The sign by the door read, "Children's Cancer Center." If I walked through those doors, I must accept a life that included a child with cancer. I wanted, rather, to turn and run. But the heavy doors were pushed open and we were escorted onto the unit and into a life we had never imagined. As the shock and denial wore off a little during those days of our initial stay, an appreciation and hope began to rise. These doctors and nurses knew what they were doing. They were smart, focused, and beyond patient with the hundreds of questions I alone asked. We were given binders and calendars and notes to help guide us. We were also given "baby steps" and told to focus on one thing at a time.

When the orthopedic doctor had said a long road of treatment stretched ahead, he was correct. The protocol for treating a boy with A.L.L. is three years and three months of chemotherapy. This also includes steroids, spinal taps, more bone marrow biopsies, and other drugs. Our plan for Karson's life never included such horrors. We thought back to the night when Karson was born, when Kraig stood by our bedside and read Psalm 139 aloud to him. Verse 16 now rang in our minds most clearly, "All the days ordained for me were written in your book before one of them came to be." On the blissful night of September 30, 2004, when we celebrated new life, we believed that God had ordained Karson's days and that He had a perfect plan for our son. Now, this diagnosis tested our faith. Did we still believe God had ordained our son's days? We grappled with this question, but we chose to cling to our faith and what we believed to be true. We continued to trust God and whatever plan He had for Karson, even though we never would have imagined or chosen cancer for our little boy.

Karson was diagnosed on February 9, 2007. When doctors informed us he would finish treatment in the late spring of 2010, we could hardly fathom that day ever appearing on the calendar.

We were starting the marathon of our lives. And we had never even trained.

*   *   *

The day after Karson's diagnosis, a doctor surgically implanted a port in his chest. The port, a porous vessel, about the size of a quarter, nestled under Karson's skin and was a small target for the needles that administered IV fluids and chemotherapy drugs. Before the port was accessed each time, we rubbed numbing cream over the surface of Karson's skin where the needles would enter. Karson felt little, if any, discomfort from the port site and this method saved the veins in his arms from constant attack. In this way, the port made treatment much easier.

But I received less than twenty-four hours to absorb this before my baby boy was taken from me and cut open for this port to be placed. The morning after his diagnosis, Kraig and I huddled in a small room in the surgery center of the Riley Hospital for Children with our parents and our only son. Karson had no idea that any minute a surgeon would put him to sleep and then under the knife.

"This is the day. This is the day," Karson sang. "That the Lord has made. That the Lord has made. I will be Joyce. I will be Joyce and be glad in it. And be glad in it." Karson's sweet little sing-song voice that couldn't pronounce "rejoice" carried through the empty hallways. Because it was a Saturday, the hospital scheduled no routine surgeries, only those that needed immediate attention, like Karson's. He sang and giggled while our hearts broke. We stood in a circle with our parents and held hands. We prayed for the surgery and for God's help with all that lay before us.

A nurse then gave Karson Versed, a conscious sedation drug. He remained awake, but very loopy and silly. When he received this same drug the day before and he had laughed and rolled his eyes around in his head, a nurse had said, "When he's eighteen and giving you that look, it won't be because of Versed, but because he's drunk!" Kraig and I only cared about her first three words. "When he's eighteen." We were desperately searching for any clue that might indicate our little boy's life would not be cut short. Her indication that he would see the teenage years gave us both hope.

Now Karson was acting like a miniature Otis, the town drunk, from *The Andy Griffith Show*. He repeated the same phrase, "Bob the Tomato," over and over in a low, throaty voice and laughed hysterically each time. We began to laugh with him. It was either that or cry. And I already had done plenty of that. Could I maybe have some Versed, too?

And then the surgeon arrived. Garbed in scrubs and composure, he eased Karson into a red wagon and pulled him away. I watched as they went down the hall, understanding the necessity of this surgery, but broken by its reality. It struck me that the port would rest near Karson's heart, leaving a permanent scar. The moment would scar our hearts as well.

When Karson awoke from the anesthesia and we returned to our room in the Cancer Center, he amazed us all by asking to play in the playroom just an hour later. The train table, complete with *Thomas the Tank Engine* trains, was calling his name. What a blessing to have it located just down the hallway. Thomas was one of the many things, both in the hospital and at home, that helped us survive. A little blue wooden train with a smiling face and colorful friends. A happy world of engines pushed down the track by a chubby little hand.

It reminded us all to just keep chugging.

*   *   *

That very evening, exactly one week after Karson started limping, Kraig and I watched in horror as drips of chemotherapy fell from a bag hanging on Karson's IV pole and flowed through clear plastic tubing into our son's body. I was lying in the bed with Karson, and Kraig was standing at Karson's left. Karson rested, quiet and still. Kraig and I looked at each other over Karson's little blond head. Together we watched those first drips of poison. Toxic chemicals flowing into our only child. Hot tears ran down my cheeks.

We never did adjust to seeing chemotherapy, and later blood, flow from a bag or syringe into our child. During blood transfusions, I'd stare at the bag of deep red blood hanging from the IV pole and I'd wonder from whose body it had come. Was it a man? A woman? Why had they given blood? What were their personalities like? What were their hobbies? I would watch the blood pass through the tube and into Karson's chest. How strange to see the blood of a stranger enter my child. My gratitude stretched beyond words for their life-giving donations, yet I ached that my son needed it.

Those first small splashes of chemotherapy on February 10, 2007 opened the floodgates for many, many more.

*   *   *

My parents had booked a couple of hotel rooms in downtown Indianapolis. For a few hours on Sunday evening, Kraig and I drove to one of the rooms and sat alone, composing an email to our friends and family. They needed to know of Karson's diagnosis and impending treatment. This occurred before the days of much social media so we communicated largely through mass emails, and soon we started a blog to share updates as well.

When Kraig typed this first email at a desk in the quiet hotel room, void of the hospital's beeps and dings to which we'd already grown accustomed, I sat beside him, quiet myself. As his fingers glided along the laptop's keyboard, he began to weep. I had seen Kraig cry a few times in our five years of marriage, I'd even seen him tear up during our time at the hospital, but nothing like this. This was the weep of a deeply wounded man. I reached out and held him as he asked, "How do you spell 'leukemia?'" Our weeping continued in stereo.

*   *   *

Though doctors released us five days after Karson's diagnosis, we did not immediately head home. The forecast called for a snowstorm.

Because we needed to have quick access to the hospital in case of an allergic reaction or the need for a blood transfusion, or worse, we decided to stay in an Indianapolis hotel until the roads cleared and proved safe. Both sets of our parents stayed with us in town and helped us to cope with this new life we'd been handed.

During one afternoon of our hotel stay, Kraig remained with Karson in our room while I took a walk through the hotel lobby and its adjoining Convention Center. I made my way into a covered walkway that stretched over a busy street. I sat on the window ledge and looked out at the snow-covered roadway where several inches of snow had, indeed, fallen. The town looked deserted. Only a few vehicles periodically and slowly ventured below me.

Wasn't this the same city that less than a week ago welcomed home its Super Bowl Champions, the Indianapolis Colts, with a ticker tape parade? Hadn't joy and celebration overflowed these very streets that now stood empty? How temporary, how fleeting life was. One day can be full of fist pumps and cheers, and the next empty and void. How quickly things can change.

When the snow quit falling, and the roads had been cleared, we made it home. But even there, home had changed.

*　　*　　*

Email sent Sunday, February 11, 2007

Family & Friends,
    On Friday morning, Christy and I were informed that our two-year-old little boy, Karson, has leukemia. We were immediately sent to Riley Hospital in Indianapolis. On Friday

afternoon Karson's bone marrow confirmed the original diagnosis and further detailed his disease as Acute Lymphoblastic Leukemia. Yesterday Karson underwent a surgery to insert a central line and port into one of his arteries in his chest. This port will be used for his chemo treatments for the next several years. He had his first chemo treatment last night and has handled it pretty well. Obviously there will be many tough days ahead for him and us. The next month is critical in that we are hoping his cancer will go into remission so that we can begin the next stage of treatment. Currently, if everything goes well, Karson will have a minimum of three years of chemo treatments.

Please pray for Karson's healing and that he will be what is considered a rapid responder. This will allow the chemo treatments to be a little less intense. Please also pray for limited side effects to all of the medication he is currently receiving. Please also pray for Christy and I (Karson is handling it much better than us.) Christy and I (and probably our parents) will have to take a class tomorrow to learn how to help administer Karson's treatments and read his blood counts. We will also learn more about what the expected side effects of his chemo treatments will be and how to best deal with them.

Ultimately, we know God is as much in control of this as He has been every other day of our lives. Obviously this is not something we would choose, but we do remain hopeful and trust in Him. We will remain at Riley at least until Tuesday and then, depending on how Karson responds to his treatments, we may be able to go home. We will be returning to Riley at least weekly for the next several months and then hopefully will be able to get *some of his chemo treatments in Fort Wayne.*

Because of everything that is going on, the education that we are receiving, and Karson's risk of any kind of infection, we ask that there be no visitors at this time. We also ask that any communication at this time be through e-mail as opposed to phone. We appreciate and will read your e-mails, but may not be able to respond. Thank you for your concern for Karson, Christy, and I during this hard time. Even more so, we would greatly appreciate your prayers. We believe we serve a big God who loves us and understands the pain of seeing a son suffer.
Thank you for interceding on our behalf.

Kraig Cabe
Northern Indiana Director
Fellowship of Christian Athletes

"For God so loved the world that he gave his one and only Son, that whoever believes in him shall not perish but have eternal life." John 3:16

life morsel: God loves me even when I don't feel it or understand.
And His love is enough.

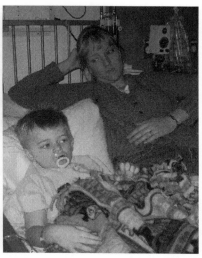

Celebrating the Colts Super Bowl victory February 4, 2007

February 10, 2007. Karson had been diagnosed the day before and had surgery this day to insert a port in his chest for chemo treatments

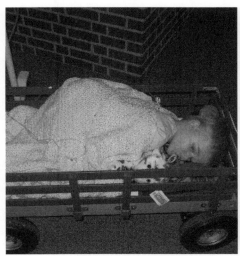

In his wagon at Riley Hospital for Children. The wagon logo is their trademark. I couldn't believe my own child was riding in one

Being comforted in Daddy's arms

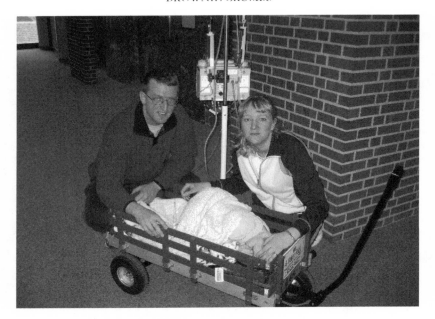

Fighting this together

Leaving Riley, but staying down town Indianapolis
because of an impending snow storm

nine

macaroni and
chicken noodle soup

why we always tried to keep both on hand

During the next three years, cancer dictated our schedule. And by schedule, I mean we had no schedule other than chemo appointments and spinal taps. We did a lot of traveling, but went nowhere. We drove 123 miles, each way, to Riley Hospital for Children at least once a week for nine months. And we continued to drive there and to our local hospital for two and a half additional years.

Kraig only missed a few chemo appointments due to work. The fact that he could come with us nearly every time blessed us tremendously. He found those rare days without us excruciating as he worked with a preoccupied mind, constantly wanting to check in for updates.

His job with the Fellowship of Christian Athletes kept him very busy, but offered flexibility. Kraig worked in the evenings after chemo days at the hospital and he rearranged his schedule in order to be with us. It caused him some extra stress, but he believed it was worth it for the season in which we were living.

Kraig's boss at the time, the one who had visited the hospital and prayed in the waiting room the day of Karson's diagnosis, was a very wise and understanding man. Tim once told Kraig a famous Jim Elliot quote, "Wherever you are, be all there." Tim gave Kraig this advice when we married and encouraged Kraig to leave work at work, to focus on FCA only at work. Kraig remembered this advice during the season of Karson's weekly chemo treatments and Tim encouraged him to be with us as long as he still accomplished the FCA work. In fact, Tim went as far as to say that being with Karson and me during this season mattered more than the FCA ministry. One day, when Kraig remained behind, Tim called him and when he heard Kraig's worried tone, he said, "If there's ever a time your family needs you, it's now. Don't miss another appointment." Kraig took this to heart.

The ministry of FCA still remained a priority to Kraig, but not his first one, and the work still got done. In fact, that first year of Karson's treatment was a very successful year for FCA despite Kraig's altered work routine.

Life looked different for Karson and me in our home routine as well. We were very isolated.

For several months after his diagnosis, Karson saw almost no one other than Kraig and me, our parents, and medical staff. Occasionally, if extended family adults were completely healthy and had not recently received any type of live vaccination or flu mist, we would allow a visit. Karson's three young cousins, who lived an hour away from us, and with whom Karson loved to play, could only communicate with him via video. The boys, ages nine, six, and two, would create videos of themselves singing, playing, and talking to Karson and send them to us in the mail or with a healthy grandparent. Karson watched their theatrical performances on repeat. He then asked us to help him make a video; we recorded him being silly and sent it back to the boys. This continued for several months.

Nearly six months into Karson's treatment, he gained enough strength for a short visit with his cousins. As we walked into the kitchen where the boys were waiting, Karson hesitated. Had our two-year-old forgotten how to play with other kids? Karson slowly approached Kordell, the oldest cousin, and gently reached out and touched his chest. At first, this confused us. Then we realized he was touching Kordell to make sure he was really there, not just an image on a screen to which he had become so accustomed. Watching Karson test the reality of the moment felt surreal.

Had it really been almost six months of living with cancer? Of isolation and a schedule dictated by blood counts?

Only the beep of a thermometer jarred us into spontaneity.

Because Karson's port catheter ran directly into his heart, any infection in it could lead to imminent death. Fever signaled a possible infection. The magic number was 100.4. If Karson's temperature hit that number, we grabbed our bags, often already packed, and headed to the Emergency Room. This happened more times during the course of three years than I can remember.

Those trips always resulted in blood work, IV antibiotics, blood cultures, and a lovely two-night stay in the hospital. I believe they also took a few months off my life. But who's counting?

When we were not in "fever mode," our new normal mode governed us. We measured out pills, crushed them, mixed the powder with liquid medications, and fed them to our child every evening and many mornings. The Walgreens pharmacy staff saw us on a weekly basis. They knew us each time I pulled up to the drive-thru window.

One evening our doorbell rang. A courier delivered a chemotherapy drug that needed to be refrigerated. It arrived in a cooler covered with bright orange stickers that read, "Caution: Hazardous Material," and "Wear Gloves When Handling." I wept as I placed it on the shelf beside our milk and orange juice. How was I expected to wear a double layer of gloves and avoid touching a toxic chemical that then must go directly into my son's body?

Spinal taps became something Karson looked forward to because he knew he'd be given his "silly medicine" (Versed) when he was taken to the procedure room. Kraig and I loathed seeing the long needle go into our son's spinal column where chemo, the color of Mountain Dew, was injected and spinal fluid was allowed to drip out. But we did enjoy Karson's surprise and delight at seeing the same tow truck poster on the wall, even after twenty-two procedures. He liked it every time! The Versed created an amnesia-like effect as he came out of the conscious sedation. Kraig and I did not have amnesia. We remember those moments well.

One evening, after we'd arrived home from a long "spinal tap day" at Riley, I was making pancakes for dinner. Karson was with me in the kitchen and I sent him to ask Daddy what he wanted to drink. Karson ran to the family room, excited to help Mommy. A thud echoed, and Kraig moaned. "Oh, Karson!"

I ran into the family room so quickly and with such fear that I literally fell onto my knees beside them. Karson had tripped over a rug and fallen headfirst into the concrete fireplace ledge. His head was bleeding. Kraig grabbed him and we hustled into our van without much discussion or decision-making. From our few months' crash course in blood work and cancer patient care, we knew that low platelets could mean Karson's body might be unable to stop the bleeding. And he was already losing quite a bit of blood.

The ten-minute drive to our local Emergency Room blurred in panicked motion. When we arrived, the staff ushered us back and Karson received four stitches near the crest of his forehead. The bleeding did stop on its own and his blood work revealed his platelet count fell into the normal range.

"I'm so thankful, but oh so tired!" I whimpered.

Kraig agreed. "Two hospitals in one day. I'm exhausted." He muttered, "I'm not sure how much further my adrenaline can carry me."

"Look at it this way," the doctor added. "When he completely loses his hair, he'll look super tough with this scar on his bald head," he joked. We agreed that he would. The scar it left on Karson still lingers, and it did enhance his "I've been through it and survived" aura. Unfortunately, the havoc the whole journey wreaked on his parents only seemed to make us appear more tired.

We ate our pancakes later that evening, looking like deer in the headlights.

Karson wore a large Band-Aid over his stitched wound and we stuck *Thomas the Train* stickers on top of it. He literally had trains on the brain for a few days. Karson was given yet another oral medicine, an antibiotic to protect his body from germs with this new and unexpected wound.

Karson also took long stints of oral steroids during the first year, which aid in the treatment of leukemia when coupled with certain chemotherapy drugs. The steroids made Karson hungry. Or should I say, the steroids made Karson *super hungry*. Never have I witnessed a small child out-eat both of his parents and then cry for more. Many nights I would get up with Karson in the wee hours of the morning and become his short-order chef when he'd plead, "I neeeeeeed mashed potatoes, Mommy!" And really, who doesn't at 2:00 a.m.?

The doctors had told us to feed him whatever he wanted while on the long steroid stints. We obeyed. Sometimes we wondered if Karson would blow up like Violet Beauregarde in *Charlie and the Chocolate Factory* and be rolled away by Oompa-Loompas, but we followed the doctors' orders and gave him what he wanted during those times. The two longest stints lasted about twenty-eight days each. Had they lasted longer, there still might be a global shortage of macaroni and cheese and Lay's potato chips.

Some of the more memorable "steroid appetite moments" involved fasting. That's right, we had to ask a child crazy with hunger to fast for a spinal tap procedure. We'd schedule our appointments for as early in the morning as we could attain them, and then brace ourselves for the two-hour drive down to Indianapolis.

One day when we were waiting to be called back, Karson literally marched up and down the hallway of the hospital yelling, "I need soup! I need soup!" Parents of other sick children snickered with understanding.

Another day, my mom traveled with us and handled "KP duty" when Karson recovered from his spinal tap and was finally allowed to eat. He asked her for chicken noodle soup, which she found in the Nourishment Room on the unit and heated up from a can. Karson ate the entire can. Mom made another. Karson ate it as well. Mom made another. This carried on until Karson had eaten nine whole cans of chicken noodle soup. The rest of us didn't know whether to laugh or throw up.

On another occasion, Kraig was the hero who found the much-needed macaroni and cheese that Karson requested after his spinal tap. Kraig carried two Styrofoam bowls full of macaroni up from the first floor to our room in the outpatient clinic.

I held the two bowls, one in each hand, while waiting for the nurse to complete the vital drills with my little trooper. In this fight against rogue cells, today I was equipped only with carbohydrates and yellow cheese. But that was enough for the moment. And hadn't I already learned, years before, that enough is all I need?

Yes, provision for today. Daily bread. Daily macaroni.

It proved tough to face tomorrow, uncertain if a fever, allergic reaction, hospital stay, or worse was to come. But it was possible to carry on if I focused on today. I simply needed to focus on accepting God's provision of daily bread.

Daily bread. And as much soup, macaroni, and potato chips as we could find.

*   *   *

Blog entry dated February 18, 2007

We have been home now for two days. Karson is doing fairly well. Kraig and I are also doing better than we ever thought possible thanks to the prayers and support of so many. We are very grateful for you all.

One thing that has brought us much-needed "comic relief" is Karson's appetite. The doctors warned us that one of the chemo drugs that Karson is taking will cause him to have an urgent and very specific hunger. They encouraged us at Riley to feed him what and when he requests (keeping in mind his low-sugar and low-salt diet.) Karson is a big guy for a two-year-old anyway and has always had a big appetite compared to other kids his age. His appetite has now been "super-sized!"

For example, Friday morning for breakfast Karson said he needed chicken. So, I fixed him chicken nuggets at 8:00am. He ate seven of them. Then, he asked for pancakes. I wasn't sure if he would have room for pancakes after all that chicken, but I made a batch and Karson ate four! Then, thinking he was done, I started to remove his bib and he said, "No, Mommy, I need soup!" Karson then washed down his chicken nuggets and pancakes with a bowl of chicken noodle soup! I'm not making this up! (In fact, as I write this on Sunday morning, Karson is on his third bowl of macaroni!)

This crazy appetite makes Kraig and I laugh and keeps us on our toes! You can pray that Mommy can keep up with the cooking and that our pantry will be stocked with the "right" foods.

Karson has been playing with his toys a lot and

watching videos. There are moments when life seems fairly normal here. There are also other moments when Kraig and I feel like we've been punched in the stomach as we are reminded of how serious this illness is. For example, each time we try to change Karson's diaper or his clothes he panics. We think maybe he is afraid that something will hurt like all of the awful procedures done at Riley.

When we gave him a bath Friday night, he screamed when he saw his little chest. Usually Karson loves baths so it was hard for us to see him so afraid. Eventually though he calmed down and did all right. Here are some pictures of Karson's port in his chest. (Note: Photos were included in original blog post.) *It is healing pretty well. Please pray that it would continue to heal and stay free from infection for the three-year duration. Also pray that Karson would not fear getting dressed or baths.*

It has still been a struggle to give Karson his medicine. We did try crushing his pill and putting it in sugar-free Hershey syrup. This helped a little but the medicine tastes awful and Karson gags as it hits his tongue. Please pray that this would get easier for us all.

I titled this blog entry " . . . and give me this minute my daily bread!" because of discussing Karson's increased appetite. But, as I think about it now, it also applies to Kraig and I. Kraig and I are praying this very statement, not for physical food, but for God's grace. When Karson is screaming and hurting and we think we can't do this another minute, we pray for just a little more grace. We can't think ahead yet to the three plus years of struggle ahead but we can do this one minute at a time. Please pray for us that God would continue to grant us His grace and patience and hope as we need it . . . day by day . . . minute by minute. So far He has been faithful to do just that.

Please also continue to pray with us for Karson's complete healing. May God bless you for your faithfulness in prayer on our families' behalf.

life morsel: "Enough" is all I need.

Karson only felt comfortable
if food was close at hand
while he was on the high
doses of steroids

Praying with Daddy after a
spinal tap to thank God for the
food he was now able to eat

Eating one of his nine cans
of chicken noodle soup after
a spinal tap. You can tell he
was greatly enjoying it!

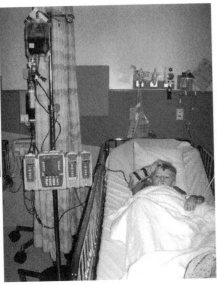

Receiving one of his
numerous blood transfusions

At Riley Hospital for Children, ready for treatment, and equipped with two bowls of macaroni

He just couldn't stop eating. He was very uncomfortable

By the end of one month of steroids, Karson's appearance had changed significantly due to the weight gain and side effects.
We had to borrow larger clothes for Karson.

ten

doughnuts and
refried beans

how both helped bring healing

A "new normal." That's what people kept telling me we'd discover. And we eventually found it hidden amongst chemo drugs and hospital corridors. It took shape within our home through medication calendars and memorized pharmacy phone numbers. Normal still existed, but it proved difficult to recognize.

We also had to establish a new normal when it came to attending church again after Karson's diagnosis. We knew Karson couldn't go with us due to the risk of being exposed to germs, but Kraig and I did plan to go back. We didn't want to simply skip church for three years. Church played a vital part of our lives. We were involved in various places and programs at Emmanuel Community and we still led the Young Adult Sunday school class every week.

We knew that our relationship with God, and even our learning and growing in God's Word, could continue without actually going to church. But we needed something else that the Church provides. Not just the Sunday morning doughnuts and coffee in the fellowship hall, though those don't hurt anything either.

I never did quite understand the meaning behind the little hand rhyme I learned as a child where you'd interlock your own hands and say, "Here is the church. Here is the steeple. Open the doors and where are the people?" You'd open your hands while keeping your fingers interlocked and reveal your empty palms. But the game wasn't over. You'd smile a sly grin and hook your hands together once again. But this time, you tucked your fingers in toward your palms as you interlocked your hands. You hid your fingers inside until it was time to turn your palms over once again. This time you shouted in mock surprise, "There are the people!" as you wiggled those silly church-attending digits in delight.

I wondered as a child if the "people" just didn't know what time church started. Maybe this was a rhyme about them always being late. Was this due to a Daylight Savings time change, or what? They seemed like knuckleheads to me.

Though an odd little rhyme, it speaks truth about the Church being full of people. Wiggly, diverse, flawed little people.

The Body of Christ, as the Bible calls it. The global community of Jesus followers.

Some of those people really are knuckleheads. But they, in their diversity and messiness, their blemishes and their potluck dinners, make up the beautiful Church.

Kraig and I needed to return to church, not to obtain a check mark by our names in the attendance database. Not to please my dad, who preached the sermons. Not to make sure we received our weekly dose of "God time" and sealed a destiny in Heaven.

We needed to return to church to be with the Church.

But as much as I needed it and knew so, I dreaded the initial return.

The day after I quit high school basketball midseason, I passed my former teammates in the hallway. The first time I saw each girl, a moment of tense eye contact occurred. Awkward. *Did they know? Had they heard? Did they understand why I quit? Would they still accept me as a friend? Did dropping basketball also mean dropping this person from my life?* I just wanted that day to end and for the final bell to ring.

As I headed to the athletic director's office where I worked during an afternoon study hall, my feet dragged. My former coach would be waiting. After a short and very awkward conversation, it was decided that maybe I should find another area in the school to serve now that I was no longer on an athletic team. I nodded and walked aimlessly down the hall with no known destination ahead. Where was I supposed to go for the next forty-five minutes of this period? What about the remainder of the semester? Where did I belong?

I wandered into the science offices where the chemistry teacher was taking his prep period. He asked what was going on, and when I explained, he offered the science department as a place to land for the rest of the semester. I never would have dreamed I'd serve in the chemistry lab. But, I did. And I did so because my world had changed. I was no longer a school athlete.

I did remain friends with my former teammates. Some of them understood my reasoning for quitting, and others did not. That was okay. What mattered was that they still accepted me for who I was, whether I wore the Viking uniform or not, and they remained friends, many to this day.

However, that awkward and painful experience stayed with me. The first day back after a life change. Now here I was again. This time with my church.

I never for one moment thought that people at church would no longer call me a friend after Karson's diagnosis. However, my life had changed and people at church pitied me for what our family was enduring. I knew they would look at me, especially initially, through the "cancer family" lens. As I saw each person for the first time, tense moments of eye contact would result. *Did they know? Had they heard? What were they told? How much did they understand? Will I ever have a conversation with them again that does not revolve around Karson and leukemia?* Time after time. Person after person. Tense

155

conversations filled the church lobby. That first morning back, I doubted if I could endure it.

But I did.

Though exhausting to return to church, I so desperately needed it. I needed those flawed people who were figuring out how to process this sudden change and who were still accepting me and loving me through it. I needed them to hug me. To pray for me. To cry with me. To make me laugh. To hand me index cards with Bible verses and forward me blog posts that spoke to my heart. I needed them to be near me and to get to know me all over again in my new normal.

The Church is the people.

"Here is the church. Here is the steeple. Open the doors, and there are the people."

There they are! Those precious, wiggly, people.

And I needed to interlock with them now more than ever.

*   *   *

We had figured out a pretty good system for attending church on a regular basis after we became cancer parents. It helped that our church offered multiple services each Sunday morning.

My mom would attend the first service and then come out to the church parking lot where Kraig, Karson, and I waited in our van in a designated parking spot. Kraig and I then stayed for the second service and Sunday school, and Mom would drive Karson back to her house.

Karson fondly remembers those "Grandma Church" days. They mostly revolve around snacks, playing video games, and the undivided attention he received from a doting adult. Who wouldn't want to join that congregation?

Kraig and I thanked God for the time together at church where we continued to lead the Young Adult class and sit through a kid-free hour of service.

One such morning, about four months after Karson's diagnosis, we were sitting in the sanctuary on the left side near the back; our regular seats. It was graduation Sunday. A service that included a tribute to the high school seniors. A slideshow complete with music and baby pictures began to play on the big screen. Photos of chubby-cheeked infants and mischievous looking toddlers scrolled by. Then the "after" pictures filled the screen. It portrayed a beautiful transformation the past eighteen years had brought to that child's life. The young men and women smiled as they posed with their cars, band instruments, or letter jackets.

I suddenly struggled to breathe. Tightness bound my chest and tears threatened to spill over and run down my cheeks. I could sense Kraig was feeling the same way.

It sucker punched us.

We were thrilled for the seniors and enjoyed seeing where they planned to attend college or work after graduation.

But the invisible question hung in the air.

Would Karson have an "after" picture?

Would he live long enough to graduate from high school?

After the service, Kraig and I stopped at the Wendy's drive-thru, like we did every Sunday after church. A little date each week, complete with burgers and fries, on the way to pick up Karson.

That day the graduation video wounded us. We both had been squashed by the invisible elephant in the room.

Over our travel fountain cups and crumpled sandwich wrappers, we talked about the rawness of our emotions. How we never knew what triggers would open the floodgates and cause the tears to flow. We talked about how painful those feelings at church had been and yet how hopeful we were.

But just like our simple date on wheels, we kept moving ahead.

*　　*　　*

I once murdered my kid brother's Mexican jumping beans. It was completely accidental, and I regretted it, but nonetheless, they died.

I had heard that the beans, which we learned were tiny moth larva in seed pods about the size of half a jelly bean, would jump more often if kept near heat. Nate owned about four or five beans that he kept in a small blue plastic case with a clear lid. We could tell when they jumped by the little pinging sound we would hear when the bean ricocheted off the plastic. The tiny larva in the bean would spasm, causing the hard shell to move. Though hardly cuddly things, and I don't remember Nate naming any of them, they were his pets, nonetheless.

One day I decided that if the beans needed heat to increase their jumping frequency then I would help them out. I may have been but a preteen, but I thought I had bean smarts.

I set the little plastic case directly on top of the lightbulb of the desk lamp in my brother's bedroom. I turned on the light. *Ahhh.* The heat from that 40 watts was palpable. I just knew that soon the beans would be bouncing with delight.

A few hours later, I checked back.

No pinging sounds. I picked up the case and inspected it. I couldn't detect any movement. So I shook the case a little. Still nothing.

I had cooked the beans. Fried those little larvae to oblivion.

Adios, Mexican jumping beans.

My heart sunk. I tried to explain my intent to Nate and that I was so sorry to have killed his "pets." He was actually pretty gracious about it considering I had committed a mass homicide.

Turns out some heat motivates the beans to jump, but a direct and unrelenting heat is detrimental.

As we walked through Karson's leukemia journey, particularly in the first year of the most intense treatment, I got a little fried myself.

I was a full-time, stay-at-home mom with a very sick, isolated child. I spent many days in hospital rooms or in my sterilized home. I was sitting directly on the cancer lightbulb. Things were getting a little toasty.

I found it interesting that during that first year of treatment, many people commented to me, either at church or through emails, that I was "handling everything so well!" Perhaps it appeared that way, but honestly, those comments bothered me because I knew the truth. On the inside, sometimes anger, fear, and frustration bubbled away. And I certainly was not trying to pretend otherwise! I was just aiming to survive, to make it through the next moment. I simply was hoping to do the best I could.

I struggled with keeping a proper perspective of fear in the early months. Oddly, I didn't fear the leukemia itself, perhaps because it was a known enemy. I feared what would attack my life next.

My life had been puttering along just fine when one day my mom died in our kitchen. I had been pregnant and happy when suddenly that child's heart stopped beating. My little blonde two-year-old was playing with his toys one day, and receiving chemo the next.

Once again I remembered the phrase, "If you hear hoof beats behind you, expect horses, not zebras." As a preteen who had lost her mother, I began to realize that zebras did, in fact, show up sometimes. Now, after my only child's startling cancer diagnosis, I watched nervously over my shoulders for the next striped beast. They kept sneaking up on me. I grew antsy.

Many nights in the months after Karson's diagnosis, I lay in bed half awake and half asleep and I'd envision something awful. Kraig falling from a cliff where I couldn't grab his hand quickly enough to save him. Or maybe I had his hand, but it slipped out of my grasp. Sometimes I saw Karson free-falling or being run over by a large vehicle. Other times a stranger wearing a lab coat told me I had a rare and terminal illness.

I didn't want the images to be there. I would cut them off in my brain and force myself to think of something else. Some nights I'd imagine one of my favorite movies, usually a romantic comedy, and I'd try to remember the scenes in the movie, "watching" it again in my head. Other times, I'd mull over a book or the latest season of *American Idol*. Anything I could do to occupy my brain so fear wouldn't roll its horror movie reel.

Sometimes these moments attacked while I was wide awake. One Sunday morning, Kraig and I were sitting in the church service. My dad was preaching. Dad apparently lost his train of thought for a few seconds and he paused for a brief moment. He almost never misspeaks or makes awkward pauses while teaching, and so my brain immediately panicked. *He's having a stroke*, I thought.

My neck and shoulder muscles tightened and I sat rigid. Dad continued to preach in front of the large crowd without skipping another beat. I was probably the only person in the congregation who noticed his initial pause.

But fear and irrational thoughts had gripped me. They held me in a vice. I froze, staring at Dad, waiting for him to collapse, or gasp for air. Instead he explained the Greek origin of a word in the verse. He pronounced foreign words and translated them while explaining their significance and applying the biblical passage to daily life. And I thought he was having a stroke. Not many stroke victims exhibit symptoms of lucid Greek translation.

But fear continued to grip me and I could not stop the irrational thoughts.

Finally, the service ended. Dad was completely fine and had been the entire time. *My* mind was out of control.

I hated these moments. I hated it when the heat of the cancer mom lightbulb burned me, squelching my ability to move and think rationally.

I needed to be near the heat. My son was the cancer patient and I never lived very far from that circumstance, but sometimes I needed to climb off the lightbulb and gain some true perspective.

Climbing off the lightbulb meant meeting a group of girlfriends at a local YMCA trail and walking in big looping circles through the park, well into the evening. Or allowing myself to be dragged to Sam's Club with a group of girls who brought me a mocha and asked if I wanted to hop in the car. Helping a lady at church teach a scrapbooking class for a few Wednesday evenings in the summer. Playing board games with my brother and his wife, Trista (Nate had married his high school sweetheart when Karson was nine months old). Nate, Trista, Kraig and I would play complex board games together, sometimes late into the night, and we'd eat snacks and laugh at our own jokes. It didn't matter if I won or lost the games, I felt victorious after those hours together.

I also tried to get off the lightbulb by watching another romantic comedy in the evening after Karson was in bed. Or a date night with Kraig at a Mexican restaurant, where I'd order my favorite meal, which included beans (refried, not jumping!)

And all of those things helped. It took discipline to take care of myself in the midst of such consuming care for someone else, but it was so necessary. Taking the steps back from the situation periodically helped me to regain control over my irrational fears and helped end the moments of panic.

The lightbulb still shone and the heat remained palpable. But, I was still alive and jumping.

I'm just sorry I can't say the same for my brother's little amigos.

life morsel: Taking a few steps back can provide a new perspective.

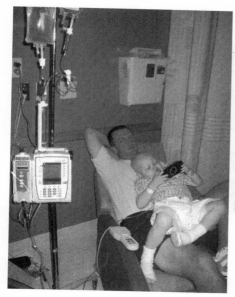

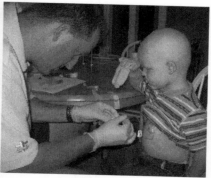

We had to be trained to give chemo through his port at home during one phase of treatment

One of the many long days of chemo

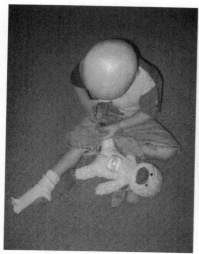

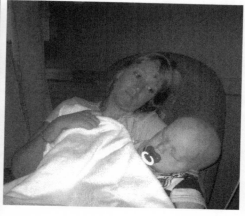

Another long day at Riley Hospital for Children

Karson "giving chemo" to his duck

Passing the time while at
the hospital

Sweet, handsome boy near
his third birthday

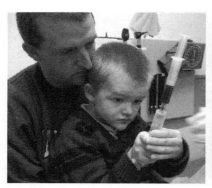

Karson loved to help the
nurses with his blood
draws. He knew the drill
well!

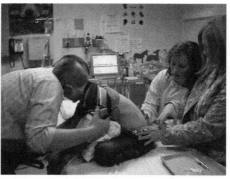

One of Karson's 22 spinal taps.
He was given a conscious
sedation drug and was awake for
each one. You can see Kraig
holding him carefully and tightly
in the correct position

eleven

breadsticks, a cup of ice, casseroles, and an apple ii

how they helped us find comfort and joy

During Karson's worst days of treatment, we did all we could to find and welcome joy. Joy can be found in times of waiting and wailing, and it can be welcomed into the pain. Granted, it may take effort to offer the hospitality, but inviting and making room for laughter, fun, and hope is always possible. Sometimes this meant taking a moment to laugh at ourselves.

Karson was in the ER with a fever and Kraig was lying on the bed with him. A blanket covered them both. My dad came in to visit and started rubbing Karson's leg. After a short while, Kraig said, "Uh, Denny. That's actually my leg." Dad jerked his hand away like he'd touched a hot oven and we all started to laugh. It felt good to laugh in the midst of such tension. I'm not sure Kraig and Dad would volunteer to repeat this moment, but the dose of comic relief proved to be a perfect prescription.

Other times we laughed at our own brain fog in the midst of so many medical terms and paperwork. We were walking around in a funk, and we weren't even the ones receiving the medication.

When filling out a medical form one morning at the hospital, I needed to write Kraig's and my names on the line. I wrote "Daddy" instead of Kraig and didn't even catch my blunder until the guy behind the desk smirked and told me I might want to be a little more specific.

Another time I was a little too specific. A nurse asked me where we'd parked in the hospital lot. We were accustomed to calling the hospital helicopter "Harold," after the helicopter character in the *Thomas and Friends* series. So when asked, I said, "We parked over by Harold."

"Oh," she said, "Who is Harold?"

I sheepishly shrugged and said, "The helicopter."

She raised her eyebrows and giggled.

Our joy often arrived in the form of a large white monorail, or People Mover, found on the campus of IU Health where Riley Hospital for Children resides. The People Mover ran on a track connecting hospitals, labs, and medical offices. It stopped at three stations within the campus.

Karson's love of trains, and his infatuation with the *Thomas and Friends* characters, led us to try a ride on the People Mover. Karson said, "I think we should name him Spencer!" Spencer was a character within the *Thomas* series, long and white and sleek, much like the People Mover. And so, we christened Spencer and he became a regular part of our lives. After each appointment, we would walk the hallways of Riley to Spencer's loading area. Karson's feet would smack sloppily against the tile floors and the noise echoed through the hallways. (One of the chemotherapy drugs that he received, Vincristine, affected Karson's walk, temporarily causing him to lose some control of his heel cords and coordination. Within a few hours, this side effect would wear off.) We'd board Spencer and ride for about twenty minutes through two stops along the IU campus before returning to our starting point. Doctors in lab coats boarded and exited and smiled at us.

One day, several family members, including my aunt and uncle, made the trip to Indianapolis with us. They stayed in a hotel and spent time with my parents, but while in town we all took time to ride Spencer. My dad created tickets on his computer that he printed for each person. They included Spencer's name, the date and each person's name. They also listed Karson Cabe as the conductor. We all presented him with our tickets before boarding. We welcomed joy into our lives that day and many other days by riding miles to nowhere on a white monorail.

We welcomed joy in other ways as well. We visited a black freight car parked along a railroad track about ten minutes from our house. We loaded into our van and drove back and forth on that road over the tracks multiples times in order to let Karson study the freight car. I didn't realize how lame this family activity truly seemed until a registration form for a MOPS (Mothers of Preschoolers) group I attended asked what we did for fun. I wrote about driving to see the parked freight car. Imagine my embarrassment when it was published in the get-to-know-our-group booklet! I doubt I convinced many others to take up our pastime, but it brought joy to an isolated little boy.

Kraig would also take Karson to our local golf course and allow him to putt on the putting green. Usually it was not a crowded place and Karson wore a mask. Both Kraig and Karson found joy in golf.

Eventually, we found joy at another hospital. Riley continued to dictate Karson's treatment, but after about a year, we were "weaned" a little and able to receive weekly chemo and blood work at our local hospital, only about ten minutes from our doorstep. Lutheran Hospital offered a pediatric oncology clinic and two pediatric oncologists, a specialty not every hospital offers. What a blessing to have these doctors and nurses, who specialized in children with cancer, so close to home!

The move away from Riley—where we had come to trust the staff—worried us a bit at first, but after a short time with the Lutheran staff, we not only gained more trusted doctors and nurses in our corner, but new friends as well.

The kids' cancer clinic at Lutheran stood newly constructed and less crowded than Riley's. The halls were wide and the rooms were comfortable. Chemo days felt almost cozy there. Karson would sprawl out on the bed and Kraig and I would "set up camp" in the room. A playroom down the hall held a variety of toys as well as an air hockey table.

But Karson's favorite part of going to Lutheran revolved around the room service. The patients in the clinic may order a meal during their clinic day by dialing a number on the long-corded phone which connected us to the hospital cafeteria. Karson, even at just three years old, would dial the number and order his meal. Most days, this meal consisted largely of carbohydrates, but no matter what else was on his menu, he always added breadsticks with cheese dip to the list. They brought Karson joy and therefore we all found joy in those lukewarm under-baked rods and fake yellow cheese sauce.

The nurses and doctors teased Karson each week and asked if he'd ordered his breadsticks for the day. We all joked that Karson might be the first person to someday take a date to the hospital for breadsticks. What a special (and understanding) girl she would have to be!

At the end of Karson's treatment, when the staff at Lutheran Hospital threw him a "No Mo' Chemo" party, they bypassed the typical bakery cake, and instead asked the cafeteria to line a nine-by-thirteen pan with breadsticks and pour cheese sauce over them for the "icing." They said it was a first, but it delighted Karson! He is still associated with breadsticks and cheese among the clinic staff.

Joy can be found in a kids' cancer clinic . . . and even ordered from room service!

*   *   *

Kraig and I worked to be intentional to have fun together as well, without Karson. This challenged us, especially in the early months of his treatment, because he demanded so much care and energy. But, as time passed, we scheduled dates and trusted grandparents to care for Karson. On one such date, Kraig and I experienced something we didn't realize we had been missing so deeply. Belly laughter.

We sat about three-quarters of the way up in a movie theater with a jumbo-size fountain drink between us. We had finished the Coke and ice remained in the cup, but my bladder was telling me it needed some attention. I wasn't thrilled about missing a few minutes of the movie in the middle of the story, but I had no choice. I quietly sneaked out of our row and started down the steps.

"Christy!" Kraig's loud whisper rang out over the actors' voices on the screen.

"Christy!" he hissed again.

I turned around and looked back at him with confusion. He was squirming in his seat and obviously trying to suppress laughter. He pointed at me.

What in the world? I thought. Why is my husband drawing attention to me needing to use the restroom?

And then I felt it.

When I had stood, the lip of the lid on our jumbo cup of ice hooked onto a button on the back pocket of my pants.

I was carrying a large, swinging cup full of rattling ice cubes on my rear end.

At this point, the other movie patrons had noticed. Snickering and pointing ensued in several rows.

I removed the cup and continued out of the theatre. And then the laughter hit. I laughed at myself the entire time I was in the restroom and as I gingerly climbed back up the theater steps to my seat. Those around us smiled at me, and Kraig squirmed with glee in his chair.

What a supportive husband!

We sat side by side and for the next fifteen minutes almost made ourselves sick trying to hold in the belly laughter that bubbled up within us.

Just when one of us would get our act together and take a deep breath, the other's shoulders would begin shaking up and down. It was a lost cause. And, unfortunately, this all happened during a very quiet, serious scene in the movie.

I had carried the burden of a jumbo cup of ice, and had not even known it. But the laughter it brought made every moment of humiliation worthwhile. Sometimes laughter heals us in places deep inside our souls.

During the course of Karson's leukemia treatments, I carried a burden with me as well. One that did not lead to shoulders shaking with laughter, but with sobbing. Kraig and I would have struggled greatly if we had to carry the burden alone.

But we were not alone. We were blown away by the family and friends who helped us in more ways than we can recall.

When we had returned from Indianapolis after the initial diagnosis stay, we returned to a collection of frozen homemade casseroles to eat at our convenience and a deep freezer in our garage that had been donated to hold them. Loved ones blessed us with meals for weeks—a huge blessing and one less thing for me to think about during the busy days of caring for Karson.

One day my doorbell rang. My friend, Rebecca, brought by a pair of new sweatpants for me. "I figured you would be wearing sweats a lot since you're staying home most of the time and I wanted you to have some new, comfortable ones." I was touched.

We began to joke that our front porch needed its own postal code, because each week a variety of items were delivered there. We found gifts for Karson, a *Thomas the Tank Engine* scrapbook with the first page started for me and many blank pages for me to complete, pizzas from Chicago delivered on dry ice, a journal with the word "Hope" written across the front, gift cards, handwritten notes, a *Thomas and Friends* t-shirt for Karson that said, "Conductor Cabe" on the back, canned food, and more.

Social media had not yet taken off, so I did not have Facebook, Twitter, or other platforms where I could keep my finger on the pulse of society and the happenings of my friends. The isolation left me out of the loop. One of my girlfriends, Amy, recognized this and began to send me weekly emails she entitled, "The Society Pages." These updates made me smile, and sometimes laugh out loud, as she humorously informed me of news she thought I'd wish to know. This ranged from the story of a mutual friend who had recently received a traffic ticket for not wearing his seatbelt in the passenger seat, to news about a girlfriend who was due with a baby any day and her antics to start labor. She was considering drinking castor oil, but hadn't yet brought herself to do it. I read the list of possible baby names for that little one, details of a remodeling project at our church, a friend struggling with her thyroid, and a couple whose water meter had burst and flooded their garage. And I was delighted to be part of it all, even if just in the reading of Amy's words. She offered me social media before its time, without the annoying political rants and recipes. These emails filled a need for me, and I loved them. She cared for my soul, and it only took a little bit of time, and an Internet connection.

Kind people met other needs as well. Someone shoveled our driveway. Our friend Diane cleaned our house once a week when we left for the day for chemotherapy treatments. She took careful consideration to keep everything that Karson would touch as germ-free as possible. She left bottles of hand sanitizer behind on our countertops as gifts.

One day we received news that an anonymous person wanted to pay the medical bills left uncovered by our insurance. We cried. We did not deserve such love and such support. We struggled to even put into words the gratitude that welled within us.

Each month Kraig painstakingly sorted insurance forms and

medical bills and tucked them into a large, three-ring binder. My dad took any bill that we needed to pay out of pocket and passed it on to the anonymous donor.

Almost three years into this routine, we received a check in the mail from the hospital for less than five dollars because our generous Good Samaritan had inadvertently overpaid on a bill. The forms listed his name. We had not meant to discover the donor's identity, but now we knew. How could we thank someone who, over the course of three years, paid more than $8,000 on our son's behalf? It was impossible to adequately thank them, but we tried. We sent the couple periodic letters with updates on Karson, and at the end of his treatment, Kraig and I took this man and his wife to dinner. We gave them a birdhouse that Karson had painted. Though a mere token compared to what they had given us, they seemed delighted.

The burden we bore when our toddler was diagnosed with cancer weighed heavily. It was almost unbearable. But because of the love and support of countless friends and family, we did not carry it alone. I kept careful records of what we were given and by whom so that I could send a thank-you note to each giver. I filled ten entire pages in my notebook with the list of gifts. I wrote a lot of thank-you notes, but they never fully expressed our true gratitude.

And the support will never be forgotten.

*   *   *

I rested alone in our bedroom on the bed and stared toward the dresser. Trinkets, loose change, and mismatched socks cluttered the polished surface. A mess. A thought struck me. What if Karson didn't live? What if we couldn't have more children? If those questions became realities, I'd no longer be a mom.

That realization shook me to the core. But oddly, it also marked a turning point for me.

No angels appeared on the dresser (too messy for them to find a seat, anyway!) and no voice boomed from Heaven. I didn't see writing on the wall or feel slain in the Spirit.

I simply knew peace.

In that moment, I knew God loved me. God was with me and always would be. I would always be Karson's mom, whether he lived long on this Earth or not. And I would spend eternity with my Heavenly Father. I also knew that eternity had already begun. Life on Earth represented just a small piece of eternity. My hope spanned a forever timeline.

The mental wrangling, the desired delay of "thy kingdom come" evaporated, and the Lord's Prayer revealed itself afresh. I realized that God's kingdom had already come. It had come inside of me. It was already here. I was living in God's presence and peace now.

Eternal life in God's kingdom had already begun.

His kingdom is yet to come on this Earth, but I can look forward to that day as well because it is all on the timeline of eternity.

That moment, staring at my messy dresser, helped me to see life truly in the light of an eternal perspective.

Years before, at one of my bridal showers, the ladies in attendance each gave me one piece of marriage advice.

One woman told me to choose my side of the bed wisely the first night because I'd likely have to sleep on that side the rest of our married life! Another told me that Kraig and I should aim to kiss each other good-bye every morning. But mostly, I remember what my Aunt Pam said. She said to always keep an eternal perspective.

It was one of those phrases that stuck intellectually in my mind. An eternal perspective.

Now, years later (while lying on the side of the bed deemed forever mine), the phrase became more than just an intellectual thought. It became real to me.

An eternal perspective.

This life on Earth is but a blip on the radar. James 4:14 says, "What is your life? You are a mist that appears for a little while and then vanishes."

Life is a season.

I had learned years earlier, after quitting basketball mid-season, that seasons do not last forever. I didn't understand that being patient and doing the disciplined work of the season could prove healthy and good. That my efforts would bear fruit. I didn't grasp that the imbalance wouldn't last forever.

That afternoon in my bedroom, I applied these truths to my most haunting questions. A sacred kind of moment where the rubber meets the road.

Life on Earth doesn't last forever.

I believe life with God, for those who accept His gift of redemption through Jesus, does.

No matter what was to come in Karson's life or my own, I knew it would be okay.

Aunt Pam's advice had moved into my heart. And it had brought with it the hostess gifts of hope and peace, no matter the season.

*   *   *

I clearly remember my little brother in our 1980s paneled-basement computer room, playing one his favorite computer games, *Karateka*, on our Apple II. He had been playing it many evenings for weeks, trying desperately to defeat all of the bad guys and advance deeper into the fortress to rescue the kidnapped princess.

One evening, Nate excitedly called us into the room as he had finally defeated the last enemy standing in his way and was ready to run into the room where the princess was imprisoned. He was about to win the game!

Nate directed the little on-screen hero into the princess's room with the controls. He made the man run to the princess. And then he used the controls to stop the hero right in front of the damsel in distress. Nate was elated! He had done it!

And then the princess kicked the hero and killed him.

Game over.

Nate began to cry. Mom and Dad and I tried to console him as we tried to figure out what had happened. Why had the princess just killed him? Didn't she want to be rescued? We later discovered the reason. If the hero character stopped in front of the princess and stood in his natural "fight ready position" which he'd been using to defeat all of the bad guys for levels and levels, the princess would assume he was there to fight her as well, and she'd strike first with the kill shot.

But, if when you defeat the final bad guy and run into the princess's room, you keep running straight into her arms, she'd welcome you into her embrace and you'd be the victor. You just had to keep running all the way into her arms.

The images from this 1980s video game endure in my mind. The running into her arms. The victory. The rescue.

Throughout my life, I've known that I am loved by God. I've grown in my relationship with my Heavenly Father and I've sung "Jesus Loves Me, This I Know." But I've often failed to run straight into God's arms.

I've stopped and stood in the fight ready position. Grappled with

God. Asked him many questions. Thrown the punches and gritted my teeth. Screamed, "Why, God?! Why did you allow this suffering in my life? When, God? When will you bring a husband into my path? How, God? How do you expect me to get through this?

And I've avoided running into His arms because I've become accustomed to the fight ready mode.

But God never delivered the kill shot.

He most certainly could. Yet He has graciously stood, arms open wide, waiting for me to embrace Him. He listened to my cries and questions and tenderly waited for me to be ready to fully accept His love.

And when I lay down my need to understand it all and allow myself to fall into his arms, His love surrounds me. When I accept the embrace without knowing the answers, then I have won. I am the victor.

Because God, in his mercy, unconditional love, and grace, has rescued me.

life morsel: We can welcome joy and host hope in the midst of pain.

The People Mover monorail
system at the Riley and IU Health
campus. We named it "Spencer"

Karson loved riding Spencer
after his long treatment days

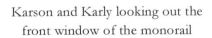

Karson and Karly looking out the
front window of the monorail

Karly was enjoying the ride!

Kraig and Karson (and stuffed animal friend, Lyle the Lamb) riding the monorail

Kraig and me enjoying a date night. We worked hard to make time to have fun together

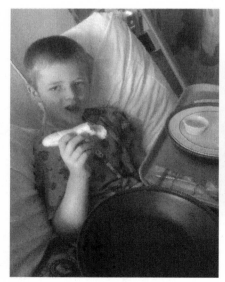

One of the many times Karson ordered and enjoyed breadsticks and cheese while at the hospital

Karson's Off Chemo Party "cake" made from breadsticks and cheese sauce "icing." The first (and only) of its kind from the staff of Lutheran Hospital's Pediatric Cancer Clinic

twelve

mold spores
and baby food

how they both invaded our life

The sudden turn of events in our lives did not derail our desire to have another child. My doctor had advised a laparoscopic surgery to help with an endometriosis issue I was having, which may have led to our previous miscarriages. So, about seven months after Karson's diagnosis, when after his second stint of steroids ended, I had surgery.

I recovered fairly easily and evidently the procedure succeeded. Within three months I was pregnant. I found myself smiling a lot in anticipation of another baby of my own to dress in footy pajamas and snuggle against my neck. But I also found myself in moments of panic that perhaps this pregnancy would end in a loss, as had the previous two. My doctor said there was no evidence that would indicate I needed to be concerned. The doctor also advised me to be extremely careful in handling any chemo drugs.

When we told Karson the news, he sweetly hugged me, but not too hard, because he did not want to hurt the baby in my belly. We knew from the start that he'd be a wonderful big brother.

My pregnancy progressed well into the second trimester, and our life began to feel somewhat manageable. That is, until water started dripping from the ceiling vent in our master bedroom. I lack familiarity with torture techniques, but I did hear about the method of dripping water onto someone's forehead in an attempt to drive him insane. Yep. The sound of dripping sporadically interrupted our thoughts and our sleep, leaving us all a little loony. Finally, I called a company that works on air ducts and they sent someone to the house.

Bad news. Our home had been built in the 1960s when baseboard heat was popular. We loved how this type of heat kept our floors so toasty, but it made our air more moist than usual due to the hot water used in the baseboard heaters. The problem arose in the winter when warm, moist air rose and met the cold air in our attic where our ceiling vents did not seal properly. Condensation began to collect in our attic air ducts and eventually puddled and dripped into our bedroom. The worst news? The pooled water that sat in our air ducts led to the growth of mold in the ducts themselves. These ducts channeled the cool air of our air conditioning unit in the summer months and blew it through our entire house. Had we turned on our air conditioning, the air in our home would have filled with mold spores.

I knew this presented a serious situation, not only for our home, but for our son. I immediately called the Cancer Clinic. They declared the problem a "medical emergency" and asked us to leave the house immediately. "With Karson's suppressed immune system," the doctor said, "a contaminant like mold in the air could be life-threatening to him."

We packed our suitcases and moved into my parents' basement. The air duct company began to replace all ducts in the attic as well as to install new ceilings in a four-by-four foot square around every vent. Though a big job, we figured we could move home in a week or two. Four months later, on July 4, we celebrated our independence once again as we left my parents' basement and returned home. I was now thirty-four weeks pregnant.

Those four months of waiting for our home to be finished were extremely difficult. I enjoyed the time with my parents, but felt aimless during the days. I could not go anywhere with Karson, and I still dealt with some morning sickness. I spent long mornings bored and purposeless as I waited until afternoon so that I could nap while Karson slept. In the evenings, Kraig and I watched reruns of *Home Improvement*—the irony of our choice dawned on us later.

When we did move home on July 4, we hardly recognized our house. The contents of our home appeared to have been placed inside a gigantic blender, taken for a spin, and then dumped randomly throughout each room. The slogan of the restoration company read, "We Restore Harmony!" I think they must have confused the word "harmony" with "haphazard."

Our curtains settled in heaps in rooms where they had not even been hanging. The hanging clothes from our closet mounded on the kitchen table and entertainment stand. Our bedding strewed over the couch, our dishes had been packed into boxes, and living room décor littered the bathrooms. Large HEPA scrubbers, that resembled small jet engines, roared. It was a nightmare.

We spent weeks putting the pieces back where they belonged. Granted, everything had been thoroughly cleaned, and for that, we thanked God. The mold was gone. The ducts shone, bright and new. I was tempted to call my friends and say, "Hey, come on over and see my brand new air ducts!" but too much work waited. Finally, just before I was due to be induced with my pregnancy, home seemed like home once again.

Our harmony had been mostly restored.

*   *   *

Even through the chaos surrounding our home improvement project that summer, Karson stayed excited to become a big brother. And he did just that on August 12, 2008, when our precious second child was born, a baby girl.

I had hoped for a girl, and when I looked into the face of my beautiful newborn daughter, her tiny pink hat tugged over her ears, my heart swelled. We named her Karly Sue.

I had always wanted a little girl so I could dress her in frilly pink outfits.

In middle school, we studied babysitting and childcare for one unit of our home economics class. My teacher expected us to "parent" a raw egg for several days. Our grades depended on keeping the egg "alive and well," unscrambled, while in our care.

I owned a little woven basket my grandparents had brought me as a souvenir from a trip to Jamaica. I emptied the basket of its usual contents, coins and junk, and lined it with tissues. It became a soft and safe egg bed. All was well.

And then the urge came over me to dress my egg in a girly outfit. Something cute and frilly, naturally. I just couldn't help myself.

I found a poufy, pink hair scrunchie. Yes, this pretty elastic band, embellished with pale pink fabric and glittering with colorful sparkles, would make a lovely egg skirt. I imagined it like a tiny tutu as it encircled my little one's shell. I couldn't wait to put it on her.

As I pulled the elastic band wide and slid my egg through it, I squeezed.

And that's when it happened. Egg parenting gone terribly wrong. My egg not only cracked, but my thumbs broke straight through the shell. Cold, wet yolk ran down my wrists.

Apparently, I was still in training and not yet ready to dress a "little one."

Now, however, as I pulled that first little pink-patterned dress over Karly's tiny body, I was ever so careful. Yet so delighted! Because this little

one was a gift far greater than any grade I'd ever receive in home
economics.

*   *   *

*Excerpt from my journal, nine months (almost to the day!)
before Karly was born:*

Tuesday, November 13, 2007

Dear Heavenly Father,

*It has been so long since I've written out a prayer.
Tonight in our quiet house I want to in order to help me focus
on you.*

*First, search me, oh God, and know my anxious
thoughts. See if there is any sin in me, and in your perfect
grace, forgive me. I do not deserve your grace and mercy that
are new every morning—every moment. Thank you, Father, for
forgiving me.*

*Lord, I love you with all my heart and live my life for
you. What peace you bring me! What comfort and love! These
last nine months, I've learned again how faithful you are, and
tender. How can you be so majestic and powerful and yet so
tender and loving? I'm so grateful, and even though I am so
saddened by Karson's illness and our struggle to have a second
child, I find my peace and joy in you. Thank you also for the
Body of Christ that has built us up and has helped to encourage
us in your name. What a blessing!*

Father, I pray you would continue to give me peace and

assurance that you are in perfect control. Show me your power in a fresh new way, Father. I believe you can. I ask you to heal Karson's body so that he will never again have to face cancer or side-effects from his treatments. I pray that you would give him a long and fruitful life for your kingdom. Use him, Father, for your glory—and I selfishly ask it be through his healthy, long life on Earth. I trust you. Yes, Father, I admit it is hard to say when I am laying Karson's life in your hand. I don't want to lose him or see him suffer further. It's so hard to think anything like that would be in your plan—but yet again, I will say I trust you. Help me, even, Lord, in my unbelief. Help me to remember the peace that passes all understanding when I lean into that trust and realize another time that it is my only choice really. How can I not trust you when you are my creator and Karson's creator? You sustain us all. Oh, what comfort!

Father, I also pray you'd give us at least one more child. We desire this soon, but again you know all things and we want your will in our lives. I lay this desire in your hands tonight as well. Do with it as you will and thank you in advance for your perfect answer.

I love you, Father. Thank you for your peace. I rest in it tonight.

In Jesus' powerful name I pray,

Amen.

*   *   *

One morning, during my stay at the hospital while I was recovering from Karly's delivery, my doctor sat across from my bed and stated that he thought we were blessed to have this second child. He continued by saying if we wanted another child we should try sooner rather than later. He suggested another surgery if we ever reached that point. "Basically," he said, "women with endometriosis like yours have small families." We understood. We knew Karly was a gift.

And so, with shock and joy we discovered I was pregnant once again, around Karly's first birthday. We still lived in the "trenches" of chemotherapy with Karson, and Karly was just learning to walk, so we knew stressful times stretched ahead. But I reminded myself what I had once learned, that just because something is not ideal, doesn't mean it's not okay. And this was okay. In fact, we felt blessed beyond measure!

*   *   *

Karly's nursery closet had been used to store some random art supplies and such, and I decided to clean it out. She needed more space to hang her ever-expanding wardrobe.

As I removed these items from her closet one evening, I noticed that the small, side wall inside the closet looked dirty. As I looked closer I saw black stains.

Oh, no. Here we go again, I thought. More mold. This time I feared it had invaded our home's structure, not just the air ducts. We already went through this struggle and we paid our time! We moved out of here for four months and spent a lot of money replacing ducts no one could see! In less than thirty seconds, I mentally played out an entire scenario of us again moving into my parents' basement. I wanted to collapse on the floor, rock back and forth, and cry. Instead, I called Kraig into the room.

He responded slightly more dramatically than I did. He went to the garage, grabbed a hammer, and hacked a hole about the size of a basketball in the wall where we saw the black stains. Behind the drywall, we found a black substance filling two feet of the space between the inner drywall and exterior wall.

Kraig began to verbally describe the same scenario I'd envisioned. Tears rose to the surface. I was supposed to leave the next morning for a much-needed weekend away with some girlfriends. Kraig declared that I'd have to stay home now. I paced the room.

Despite the late hour, we decided to reach out for help. We needed someone else to come into our situation and intervene. Panic and dread were blinding us to reality and hope.

Kraig called my dad. "Denny, can you come over here? We found something in Karly's closet that we think is black mold. Can you just come look at it?" Dad arrived within fifteen minutes.

I put Karly to bed in another room and came back in to watch Kraig and my dad investigate. After a few minutes, Dad said, "I don't think this is mold, guys." Kraig and I were still taking deep breaths and trying to get a grip. "Look in here."

We shone flashlights and carefully inspected the small crevice in the wall. Inside, we found the black substance only in the one area where Kraig had made the hole. The exterior wall on the other side of the mess butted up against our landscaping and mulch bed. After Dad explained, and we took time to let a new scenario sink in, we determined that a rodent of some sort must have burrowed into the ground and laid a nest between the walls. The black substance turned out to be the fecal matter left behind.

"It's just rodent poop!" Kraig exclaimed as if we'd won the lottery! Breath filled my lungs and then burst out of my mouth. We could easily clean this and cover it with a new piece of drywall!

We hugged and high fived and thanked my dad repeatedly for coming. When blinded by our fears, we needed Dad to truly study the evidence and help us see reality.

With the problem resolved, I was able to go on my getaway weekend the next morning.

Never have rodent droppings been such a piece of good fortune.

* * *

It was the day before my birthday, but instead of throwing a party, Kraig was holding his annual fundraising banquet for the Fellowship of Christian Athletes. Each year, in addition to FCA ministry updates, donor guests enjoyed hearing a well-known athlete or coach share a keynote. This year's banquet would top them all. Legendary football coach, Tony Dungy, who won a Super Bowl with the Indianapolis Colts in 2007, would be the keynote speaker. The banquet hall filled with about 1,500 Hoosiers, many of them adoring Colts fans. Dungy delivered a powerful and encouraging message.

But in the hours before he stood on that stage and spoke about his faith, Dungy had stood with us in the hallways of the Pediatric Cancer Clinic at Lutheran Hospital.

Knowing that Dungy, who now was coaching in Tampa, Florida, used to visit very sick children at Riley Hospital for Children in Indianapolis while coaching the Colts, Kraig asked if he would do the same in our city before the banquet. Dungy generously agreed.

We worked with the Child Life specialists at Lutheran Hospital to arrange for the families of children currently fighting cancer to be at the clinic, a few in each patient room, during the timeframe we would be bringing Dungy. It went as planned, and Dungy graciously moved from room to room, chatting with the families and showing true concern and care for each child and situation. In fact, Kraig began to sweat, because as he looked at his watch, he noticed that we needed to leave to arrive at the banquet on time. Dungy understood, and we made it to the event on time, but Dungy never acted hurried. In fact, in a calm and gentle manner, he gave each family his full attention.

"It stressed me out today at the clinic when we were pressed for time." Kraig confessed to me later. "But, I want to love others like Dungy modeled today. I want to be gracious with people like he was." I agreed.

Later that evening, after the guests left and Dungy's plane flew him toward home, Kraig and I, and some other FCA staff members, exhaled a deep breath as we helped clean the banquet hall.

"How do you think it went?" Kraig's boss, Tim Johnson, asked.

"It was good." Kraig said. Then he began to list several small things that didn't go exactly as planned. After listening a few minutes, Tim stopped him and said, "Kraig, if it had gone any better, it wouldn't have mattered. What I mean is, it went so well, those mistakes didn't make a difference."

I kicked the shoes off of my swollen feet and sat. Eight months pregnant and tired from a long day, I let the weight of what Tim said sink in. I liked the sentiment; if it had gone any better, it wouldn't have mattered. The idea of enough being truly enough was being reiterated in my life. There could always be more. There could always be something that could have gone better. There could always be more tasks accomplished and people served. There could always be more, better, grander. But at some point, more is not more. Enough is truly enough.

*   *   *

I rubbed my large belly and piled cookies on a platter. Less than two weeks away from my due date with baby number three, we were hosting a party. A celebration of a journey's end. We had spent part of the week sleeping at the hospital as Karson fought off yet another fever and a skin infection called impetigo, but now we were home with our gathered families. The spring of 2010 had arrived on the calendar, after all.

As a child, I learned that the tunnels on the Pennsylvania Turnpike eventually ended. Our car emerged from the darkness of the tunnel and burst into the light of day. The Cabes now neared the end of the leukemia journey. We could so clearly see the light at the end of tunnel and we headed toward it. When the brightness of day hit us, we knew we'd need to squint for a while. But that was to be expected. We had been in the tunnel for a long time.

Karson had taken his last dose of chemotherapy the day before, April 23, 2010. This evening he could eat dairy products, which had been restricted each evening during the chemo. Karson requested a "cookies and milk party" to celebrate. We had milk: vanilla milk, chocolate milk and strawberry milk, and plenty of cookies to help wash it down.

We had placed all of Karson's oral medications on our island counter. We pulled our large blue kitchen trashcan to the center of the room. One by one, Kraig held up a bottle of medication and shared with us all the yucky side effects it had caused. "This one made you itchy, Karson."

Karson grabbed the bottle and slam-dunked it into the trashcan. It took several minutes to complete this beautiful trashing ceremony, and I choked back the tears as I watched. Those medications shared in our daily lives for more than three years. Now they lay piled on top of each other in the garbage can. A strong visual that we were emerging into the sunlight after the leukemia tunnel. I could feel the heat of the sun and I liked it, yet it made me a little uncomfortable as well.

A thread of uncertainty wove through me, not knowing if Karson would remain cancer-free without the daily use of the drugs. Did we still need them? Were the doctors sure we could stop treatment? Had we done enough?

What would life hold as we re-emerged into society and accepted invitations to playdates with germy children? How would we adjust to soon becoming a family of five?

On the other hand, the warmth and hope at the end of tunnel called to me. It looked so inviting. Dare I enjoy it?

Yes. I dared.

There would be times of squinting and squirming as we adjusted to the changes. There would be difficult transitions and moments of anxiety and confusion. But mostly, we could enjoy the many blessings in our lives. We could live in deep gratitude for the answers to prayer, answers we could reach out and touch with our hands.

A verse I had clung to, and even made the signature at the bottom of all of my emails for years during this season, was 2 Corinthians 1:10b-11: "On him we have set our hope that he will continue to deliver us, as you help us by your prayers. Then many will give thanks on our behalf for the gracious favor granted us in answer to the prayers of many."

Many had indeed prayed on our behalf. Many now gave thanks on our behalf, as well. And the pile of medication in the trash can, the cookies and milk on the table, and the wriggling baby in my belly reminded us that we had indeed been granted amazingly gracious favor.

*　　*　　*

Email sent April 23, 2010

Family & Friends,

On Sunday, February 11, 2007, many of you received the email I copied below informing you that our then two-year-old little boy, Karson, had been diagnosed with leukemia. Needless to say I think we typed that email while still in a state of shock. However, tonight I am excited to share that on Monday, Karson received his last chemo treatment at the hospital and tonight he took his last chemo pill! The past three years, two months and fourteen days have not always been pleasant for Karson (consider the three bone marrow biopsies, twenty-two spinal taps, over 100 blood draws, nightly chemo medicine, and countless trips to Lutheran and Riley), but he has remained in remission and his body continues to respond really well to the treatment. The next year will be critical to determine if his body can remain cancer-free on his own (as opposed to chemo-assisted as it has been for the past three years), but we are extremely grateful to be where we are tonight and his prognosis is very good!

Christy and I just wanted to write and thank each of you for your prayers, the encouraging words, notes, cards & emails, and the general support we have received.

This morning, in the course of my normal Bible reading schedule, I read from John 9. Here is a portion of the passage I read: 'His disciples asked him, "Rabbi, who sinned, this man or his parents, that he was born blind?" "Neither this man nor his parents sinned," said Jesus, "but this happened so that the work of God might be displayed in him.' (v. 2-3)

While I don't claim to know what lies ahead for Karson, I do believe that the work of God has been displayed in his young life.

Thank you for praying for Karson and the rest of our family! As always, if you want more of the details, or if you would like to see pictures, you can go to Karson's blog.

May the Lord bless you for the kindness you have shown to our family through this season of life!

Celebrating!

Kraig, Christy, Karson, Karly (and baby #3 . . . due any day!)

*   *   *

One week later, April 30, 2010, Kraig and I drove to the hospital once again. This time for a joyfully anticipated scheduled procedure—an induced delivery of Cabe baby number three.

We pulled into a parking spot in the hospital lot as the sun was rising. Kraig parked the van. The two of us sat alone and quiet for a moment, then Kraig reached over, grabbed my hand and began to pray aloud for the day ahead. As he prayed, the sunlight grew brighter as the day dawned around us. Through my closed eyelids, the light shone. The sun's warmth fell on my face. And immediately, the words of Numbers 6:24-26 played in my mind.

They were the same verses that had impacted me earlier in life as a kindergartener, camping in the back yard, who wanted her father's face turned toward her. The same verses that brought me peace and understanding as a parent watching my only son turn his face toward his daddy, looking for help and love as he was being pinned down on a procedure table. The same verses that now seemed to shine directly into my soul as I sat in a hospital parking lot ready to deliver my third child.

"The LORD bless you and keep you; the LORD make his face shine on you and be gracious to you; the LORD turn his face toward you and give you peace."

Tears sprang up behind my eyelids. Peace. Gratitude. Joy. Hope. The emotions flooded me.

God's presence warmed me even more than the sun on my cheeks and nose. I sniffled and said, "Amen!" when Kraig finished his prayer.

We walked into the hospital together, anticipating a new life about to begin.

*   *   *

The five of us were together for the first time. The grandparents had brought Karson and Karly to the hospital to see their new little sister. Everyone waited for their turn to hold our newest family member, a beautiful baby girl.

We gave her the name Kenzie Grace. Kenzie because we liked it, and Grace because we couldn't have chosen a better word to represent her presence and timing.

Grace had brought us this new little life. Grace had carried us through the past three years.

And grace will remain until "Thy kingdom come!"

life morsel: Gratitude and grace grow when given without restriction.

Karson couldn't wait to be a big brother. He wanted to name the baby "Larry Pickle." We went with Karly, instead

This was the state of our kitchen when we were able to move back home. Utter chaos! We cleaned it up and got settled as quickly as possible before the baby was born

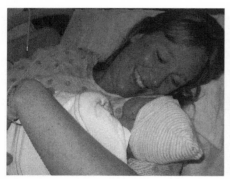

She's here! A little girl

I was so excited to dress a little girl in all the pink and frilly clothes and accessories

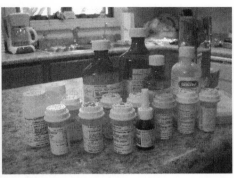

Some of the medications
Karson took for three years

At the Pediatric Cancer
Clinic at Lutheran Hospital
with guest, Tony Dungy

Enjoying his Cookies and Milk party

Slam dunking into the
trashcan the medicine he
was now done taking!

Here we go again! Another baby is soon to be born. Karson hoped
for another sister. He got his wish

Together for the first time as a family of
five when Kenzie Grace was born.
What a day!

epilogue

coffee and mercy

why I need both every morning

I stood in the hallway of the hospital. My youngest child, five-year-old Kenzie, sat on the playroom floor. Karson and Karly were at school, in the fifth and first grades, respectively. Kenzie and I were spending a Tuesday at the Pediatric Cancer Clinic at Lutheran Hospital helping a friend whose two-year-old daughter was fighting the same type of leukemia Karson had fought.

Karson visits this clinic only once a year now, for blood work and physicals to check his health. He's not required to be looked at medically more than yearly because he's now been off chemo for five years, and though he'll never be declared "cured," he is cancer-free and completely healthy. He is the tallest eleven-year-old in his class, which makes us smile, because the oncologist had previously told us that the chemotherapy would likely stunt his growth. Karson is strong and smart. He pitches for his Little League baseball team and plays center on the basketball court. Thankfully, he's more coordinated and athletic than his mom ever was! No one would believe by looking at Karson that he spent his toddlerhood sickly and bald. His annual checkups have never even revealed a negative side effect remaining from all of the toxic drugs. God spared his life, first in my womb all those years ago, then from cancer. Now he is not only surviving, but thriving.

I am thankful for the opportunity to be at the clinic and help carry another's burden, because I remember how very heavy it is. Kenzie looks forward to the days she can play with her friends at the clinic and bring smiles to their faces. It's truly a win for all.

And then there's Kelly.

Kelly is our neighbor's dog. Our neighbor brings her to the clinic every Tuesday to visit the sick kids. In fact, I see Kelly at the hospital more often than I see her across the yard.

Today as Kenzie and a friend pet Kelly, who is wearing pink beads on her furry head, I chat with my neighbor lady and the volunteer accompanying her.

"So you literally live right by each other?" the woman asked.

"Yes, we do!" my neighbor answered. "In fact, when her kids swing on their swing set, I can hear the chains creaking every time."

"Oh, I'm sorry!" I stammered. "I know our swings are so creaky. I'm sure it is annoying. We'll have to oil them."

"Oh, no! Please don't," she said with a smile.

Later that evening I mentioned the conversation to Kraig. "Isn't it funny she doesn't want us to oil the swings? It's like she enjoys the sound."

"I bet she does," Kraig said. "It's the sound of life being lived. Kids playing on their swing set. I'd say that's a pretty good sound."

Life being lived. Yes, I'm a fan.

Some moments of my life have been harder to swallow than others, but, overall, I've savored most.

Each evening the sun sets. Sometimes it's closing out a bitter day, and other times it is the cherry on top of a sweet one. But every morning, a new day begins. I choose how to live it.

My mornings always begin with a cup of coffee. Okay, two. It's a habit, but I simply love the taste. I think about coffee when I wake up and I look forward to holding the warm cup in my hands.

I also think about mercy. Thank goodness it's served up fresh every morning as well. Without it, the bitter days would never be redeemed and the good days would never be appreciated.

Lamentations 3:21-23 says, "Yet this I call to mind and therefore I have hope: Because of the Lord's great love we are not consumed, for his compassions never fail. They are new every morning; great is your faithfulness."

The crumbs I've savored have been a wonderful feast.

à la carte

reflection/discussion questions

Prologue

Brownie Crumbs

- Do you strive to savor life through heartache, joy, and the moments in between? Why or why not?

Chapter 1

Animal Crackers

- What was your experience with church and Sunday school as a child?
- What did you learn about God as a child? Do you still believe it to be true? Why or why not?
- Describe a time in your life when the idea that "just because something is not ideal, doesn't mean it is not okay," rang true?
- As a child, a dog attacked me and left a scar above my eye. I let go of being afraid, and therefore, I did not grow up with a phobia of dogs. What fears do you cling to because of a painful incident in your past?
- What does Numbers 6:24-26 mean to you? "The Lord bless you and keep you; the Lord make his face shine on you and be gracious to you; the Lord turn his face toward you and give you peace." Have you ever experienced what you would describe as the Lord's face turned toward you?

Chapter 2

Deli Ham

- Have you ever lost a loved one to death? How do you help yourself hold on to special memories of your loved one?

- I believe that the death of Jesus on the first Good Friday offered a way for my life to be redeemed, for my sins to be forgiven, and for me to spend eternity with God. Do you believe this? If yes, do you live like you believe it? If you don't believe this to be truth, why not? Be specific.

- Have you ever received a "careless" comment from a well-intended person during a difficult time in your life? How did you respond?

- Have you ever said something hurtful (unintentionally) to someone who was struggling? How may your words have been painful? What did you learn from that experience?

- Do you believe that God is good, even when bad things happen? Why or why not?

- How have you experienced God's "strength for today?"

- Do you have "hope for tomorrow?" On what is your hope based?

- How do you handle change and transition in your life? Describe a time that you experienced a lot of change at once. How was it a good thing or a bad thing?

Chapter 3

Cereal for Supper

- I decided to love another mom instead of letting death have the final word. Have you ever opened your heart to a new love or idea that was not in your original plan? What helped you to be open to this new love or idea? If not, what is stopping you from being open?

- How can you tangibly help someone in need, like the ladies at my church helped me? Who in your life is hurting that may just need to spend time with you? Do you notice the pain of others? Do you try to do something to make it better?

- My classmate and I were both called to the guidance counselor's office in hopes that we would share in each other's pain as we talked about the similar losses of our mothers. We were unsure what to say. Who in your life is experiencing a struggle similar to one you've been through or are going through? How can you encourage him or her?

Chapter 4

Gatorade and Daily Bread

- Participating in sports taught me valuable life lessons—win or lose. What is something you have learned from playing sports or from another hobby?

- Have you ever felt overwhelmed by your life/schedule? What do you do to gain much needed perspective?

- Do you trust God for "daily bread?" How do you make this a habit in your life?

- In what ways do you try to "store up" for tomorrow? How can you break this habit and trust God instead in the present?

Chapter 5

The Dish

- If you are single, do you pray for your future spouse? If you are married, do you pray for your spouse on a regular basis? What reminders can you put in place in your life to help you be more consistent with this?

- If you are married, ask your spouse how, specifically, you can pray for them. Write it down. Pray.

- If you are married, do you pray with your spouse? If not, what practices could you put into place to start making this a habit? If you are single, do you have a friend that you can pray with about your deepest longings and needs? If not, what can you do to seek out such a friend?

- Are you striving to live a life that honors God, no matter what? Do you trust God with your future? Why or why not?

Chapter 6

Humble Pie and Wedding Cake

- If you are single, what are three qualities you can pray for in a future spouse (if you desire to be married)? If you are married, what are three qualities you appreciate in your spouse? Tell your spouse.

- Have you ever had to let go a dream (like when I tried to move on from Kraig)? What was that dream? Has God since given you the desires of your heart? If so, thank Him today. If not, what new dream is He leading you toward?

- When have you showed kindness to someone even though you did not believe they were showing kindness to you? How did this make you feel?

Chapter 7

Dark Chocolate

- What bittersweet times have you experienced in your life? What made them bitter? What made them sweet?
- Have you ever experienced a miscarriage or infertility? How have you allowed yourself to grieve the pain of miscarriage or infertility? Why or why not?
- What does "It is what it is" mean to you?
- When were times you allowed yourself to walk through grief instead of around it? How have you faced your grief head on? How have you avoided grief in hopes it would go away?
- How can you care for someone who is grieving today?
- When have you selfishly held back in prayer?
- Talk about the kingdom of God. Can it mean more than just Christ's return?
- Do you yearn for Christ's return? How often do you think about His second coming? How often do you pray for His return?

Chapter 8

An Asparagus and Chemotherapy

- How have you responded when you or a loved one experienced a shocking diagnosis?

- When have you cried out to God in anguish? Or, what stops you from crying out to God?

- During Karson's painful bone marrow biopsy, he looked to his daddy for comfort. Have you ever looked to God for comfort? If so, what was the result? If not, why not?

- God's love is enough to sustain us. Do you know and feel God's love? How have you recently experienced God's love?

- Karson innocently sang a song about rejoicing in the day—the day Lord had made—even though it was one of the worst days of our lives. When have you tried to rejoice in the midst of sorrow? What was the result?

Chapter 9

Macaroni and Chicken Noodle Soup

- During the days of intense chemo and the fears of fevers, we lived in isolation. The thermometer and Karson's cravings dictated our lives. What things dictate your life?

- What will you need to reorder to bring your life back into alignment with God?

- Can you find humor, even in the darkest of moments? Why or why not?

- The Jim Elliot quote that Kraig's boss shared with us is something I try to live by every day: "Wherever you are, be all there." What does this quote mean to you?

- How do you feel about sharing your needs, whether physical or spiritual, with others? Do you allow others to intercede in prayer on your behalf? Why or why not? Who, specifically, do you share your needs with on a regular basis?

Chapter 10

Doughnuts and Refried Beans

- Has the Church (the people!) ever rallied to help you during a time of need? How did it make you feel? In turn, how have you tangibly served someone else in need?
- Just as I needed to sometimes "climb off of the lightbulb" during the most difficult season of our cancer journey, in what areas of life do you need to step back and gain health or perspective? How can you do this? Be specific.
- Do you experience anxiety? Fear? Irrational thoughts? What steps can you take to deal with these?
- Will you bravely take the next needed step in your life to share with a trusted friend something you've been unwisely keeping to yourself?

Chapter 11

Breadsticks, a Cup of Ice, Casseroles, and an Apple II

- How can you welcome joy into trial? How can you overcome a struggle with this?
- Describe a recent time when you belly laughed.
- How would you define "living with an eternal perspective?"

- Based on your definition, do you live with an eternal perspective? What would help you gain an eternal perspective when you are struggling?

- Do you more often stand in the "fight ready position" and question God, or more often fall into His arms and accept His love?

- What things are you "fighting with God" about right now?

- What would it look like for you to fall in God's arm and accept His love?

Chapter 12

Mold Spores and Baby Food

- Describe a time when you prayed specifically for something and saw God answer in an amazing way.

- Do you pray specifically on a regular basis, or do you "robotically" go through the motions of prayer? What needs to change in your prayer life?

- How do you celebrate life's victories? We celebrated the end of Karson's chemotherapy by allowing him to throw away his bottles of medicine. We also indulged in abundant cookies and milk as a way of rejoicing. How do you celebrate the accomplishments of others? Do you acknowledge the goodness of the Lord in these moments?

- John 9:2-3 reads, "His disciples asked him, 'Rabbi, who sinned, this man or his parents, that he was born blind?' 'Neither this man nor his parents sinned,' said Jesus, 'but this happened so that the work of God might be displayed in him.'" How is the work of God displayed in you?

- As the sun shone on my face the morning of Kenzie's birth, Numbers 6:24-26 again came to my mind. "The Lord bless you and keep you; the Lord make his face shine on you and be gracious to you; the Lord turn his face toward you and give you peace." Have you ever experienced what you would describe as the Lord's face shining on you? When? How would describe this to someone?

- How would you define the word "grace?" Describe a time when you experienced grace.

Epilogue

Coffee and Mercy

- Coffee is something that I enjoy that comforts me daily. What is something "earthly" that comforts you and brings you delight?

- How would you define mercy? Describe a time when you experienced mercy.

- Lamentations 3:21-23 says, "Yet this I call to mind and therefore I have hope: Because of the LORD's great love we are not consumed, for his compassions never fail. They are new every morning; great is your faithfulness." Do you believe God's compassions (His mercy) are new every day? If so, how does this encourage you? If not, why not?

- What is one thing you have learned about God and/or His word that will help you to savor life's crumbs?

life morsels

1. Just because something is not ideal doesn't mean it is not okay.

2. When change rocks your world, when death stings, live anyway. God offers strength and hope for the living.

3. Sometimes loss offers us unexpected blessings.

4. Tomorrow's peace can't be bottled today. It won't stay fresh.

5. Enjoy today. Pray about tomorrow.

6. Love is a gift. Give and receive it freely.

7. Grief is what grief is. Acknowledging pain helps bring healing.

8. God loves me even when I don't feel it or understand. And His love is enough.

9. "Enough" is all I need.

10. Taking a few steps back can provide a new perspective.

11. We can welcome joy and host hope in the midst of pain.

12. Gratitude and grace grow when given without restriction.

acknowledgements

Writing a book is no small task, especially for someone who has never done it before. Sure, I've dabbled in blogging and I've written Bible curriculum for kids, but this is different. This is my story. This is my life. This is a full-blown project that took years to complete. And I most certainly did not do it alone.

Writing these acknowledgments may be one of the most difficult parts of writing this book. Seriously. How am I supposed to thank everyone who has made my life story possible? What if I forget someone? How do I put my deepest love and appreciation into an 11-point font?

I will do my best.

I'll start with those who helped guide the technical aspects of this project, and I'll end with those who have helped guide my life.

To Dr. Dennis E. Hensley, and Jaci Miller, who read my words with such care and craft that they sharpened me as a writer with each thoughtful edit. Thank you for your attention to detail and for helping me with the "mechanics" of this manuscript. And, Jaci, your kinds words and your prayers for me in the midst of split infinitives and too many uses of the word "apparently," mean a lot to me! You both have made me a better writer. Apparently.

To Reusser Design, thank you for taking the time to teach me about hashtags and websites (even though I still don't fully understand either!). Your kindness and expertise is a blessing to me and will help get the message of God's love and hope into the hands of those who may be encouraged by it.

To Steven Camp, who agreed to film and edit my book trailer even though he originally had never heard of a book trailer and didn't know where anyone would watch one. Regardless, we made one and I love the result! Thanks for putting up with my weird ideas and requests (like, can we use a drone in a cemetery?)

To Susan, thank you for designing such a beautiful cover for this book. I also appreciated your smart design suggestions for the book interior. You are such a joy to work with! Thank you!

To Paul Batura, thank you for believing in me and the message I'm sharing. Your support and assistance with Mr. Daly's endorsement mean an awful lot to this "rookie."

To Colleen Coble, who not only responded to a stranger's (my) request to meet her for coffee to talk about writing and publishing, but invited me to her house and served me "good coffee" over a wonderful chat. Your support and mentorship has been a blessing to me. Thanks you for writing the foreword to this book. And, thank you for your kindness and humility.

To my church family. My how you've grown over the past twenty-eight years! I guess you could say we've grown up together. I'm so thankful to call ECC "my church" and for all the love, support, and friendships that you've blessed me with.

To my writing group girls, Lori and Sara. I'm so grateful for the hours we've spent together pouring over pages of our written words. Those paragraphs represented our lives, our stories, our hearts. Thanks for listening to mine and for your delicate care in shaping my craft, while at the same time, challenging me to improve. And thank you for trusting me with your words as well. It has been an honor.

To my family. You are all the best. From my grandparents, to my aunts and uncles, to my wonderful in-laws. I have such a supportive and fun gang of people I can call my own. How did one girl get so lucky?

Thanks to my in-laws, Lee and Melody, for raising the man I love and for also loving me. Thanks for consistently asking me, "Anything new with the book?" and for supporting me throughout this process. And actually, thanks for supporting me in everything over the years. I love you guys!

To my Pappy Miller, thank you. Thank you for being the sweetest proofreader I've ever known. I'm sorry you had to use so many tissues in the proofreading of this book. But, I'm so grateful that you read it (was it four times?). I know Grandma was nosy and read it early too (I wouldn't have wanted it any other way!) and I'm so happy you both did. I love you!

To my one and only sibling, my favorite brother, Nate. My life has been more fun because of you. What's the phrase you coined for someone who exponentially changes everyone's mood for the better? A "fun multiplier?" Well, you are one. And I'm so grateful for your friendship as well as the laughs. Love you, bro. And oh yeah, sorry about those jumping beans.

In loving memory of my mom, Mary, who helped lay the foundation of my life for almost eleven years. She was kind, gentle, wise, patient, and godly. She loved God and His Word and was a great teacher. She helped in my school classrooms, took me to the library for summer reading programs, and loved me well. I hope this book honors her legacy.

Mom (Karin), it's so hard to put into words what you mean to me. When I sit back and think about the way God brought you into my life and how we've been friends ever since, as well as mother and daughter, it makes me weepy. What love, grace, and humility you possess. I love you very much and pray you are honored by the way I tell this story.

Dad, if you haven't noticed, your influence on me is pretty remarkable. The ways you taught me, led me, and loved me are all over these pages. We've been through a lot together, and I believe we've come out stronger because of it. I'm forever grateful to call you not only my dad, but also my pastor, and my friend.

Kids, at the printing of this book you are ages 12, 8, and 6. I wish I could freeze time right now. I love this stage of parenting. But honestly, I've loved every stage. You three bring me so much joy! I always wanted to be a mom some day, but you've made it better than I ever even imagined. And hey, Mommy finished her book! Yay! Thanks for believing in me and cheering me on as I've work on this! I hope that some day you'll read it. You guys are the biggest reason I wrote it.

Kraig, where do I even begin? First of all, even though you initially gave me back that Christmas ornament I made for you before we dated, I still love you more than you could ever know! I set a high standard for a husband, and you have easily exceeded it. You are one of the best blessings I've ever been given. Thank you for believing in me as I've worked on this project. Thank you for proofreading paragraphs when I requested, and then being kind to me in return when I got defensive over your edits. Thank you for listening to the hundreds of hours of ideas, concerns, vision, excitement, and panic that came out of my mouth as we dreamed about this project together. Thank you for leading our home in such a godly manner. Our themes have been peace, joy, hope, and God's faithfulness. I like that. Thank you for loving me the way you do. I love you, babe!

And finally, I'm grateful to the Lord for giving me this opportunity. I not only dedicate this book to Him, but my life. May the words on these pages, and the thoughts and actions of my days glorify my Father in Heaven who has graciously turned His face toward me and given me peace.

ABOUT THE AUTHOR

Christy Cabe writes about life through an honest, observant, and down-to-earth voice. She has been known to make her readers cry and laugh within the span of a few moments as she focuses on truth, hope, and humor. Christy enjoys telling a good story in hopes that the reader will walk away encouraged and inspired to grow in their love for God, and for others. She has a degree in educational ministries from Huntington University, drinks coffee every morning, and lives in Indiana with her husband, Kraig, and their three children.

You can find Christy's blog at christycabe.com

97155444R00140

Made in the USA
Columbia, SC
13 June 2018